The Eggplant Cookbook

The Eggplant Cookbook

*Classic and contemporary recipes
for today's healthy diet*

Rosemary Moon

CHARTWELL
BOOKS, INC.

A QUINTET BOOK

Published by Chartwell Books
A Division of Book Sales, Inc.
114, Northfield Avenue
Edison, New Jersey 08837

This edition produced for sale in the U.S.A.,
its territories and dependencies only.

ISBN 0-7858-0896-5

This book was designed and produced by
Quintet Publishing Limited
6 Blundell Street
London N7 9BH

Creative Director: Richard Dewing
Art Director: Silke Braun
Designer: Rita Wüthrich
Project Editor: Diana Steedman
Editor: Alexa Stace
Photographer: Iain Bagwell
Food Stylist: Lucy Miller

Typeset in Great Britain by
Central Southern Typesetters, Eastbourne
Manufactured in Singapore by Pica Colour Separation Overseas Pte Ltd.
Printed in Singapore by Star Standard Industries Pte Ltd.

Contents

Introduction

The eggplant is one of the most popular Mediterranean vegetables, and there is an increasing number of culinary enthusiasts, eager to experiment with this delicious vegetable.

Rounded and smooth, the most common varieties of eggplants range in color from deep purple to pink, and often weigh upward of one pound. Roasted, baked, or fried, they are the main ingredient in countless dishes, but can also be used as an extra, to turn an ordinary dish into something special. Eggplants marinate well, and readily absorb the flavors of seasoning and spices. It is simply not true that all eggplant dishes contain vast amounts of oil and must therefore be greasy. Many dishes can be almost fat-free if the eggplant is broiled or barbecued in preference to being fried. I still remember the delight and pleasure when I first tasted a broiled eggplant. The flesh assumes a glorious smokiness, a subtle flavor that can be savored on its own, or used as a delicious background for dips and sauces. This flavor is even more pronounced when the eggplant is cooked over the barbecue, preferably over wood chips.

Above *The exquisite, white Ova variety clearly suggests how the eggplant got its name.*

Right *Slim Jim – an excellent eggplant for slicing.*

Eggplants Worldwide

Many cuisines around the world feature eggplants, but it is Chinese, Greek, Turkish, Italian, Indian, and Thai dishes that are especially associated with them and are a mainstay in their cooking.

China

Chinese dishes often include braised eggplants, and they are especially used by the numerous Buddhists who follow a strict vegetarian diet. Most Lo-han recipes in particular, which originated in the monasteries of China and Tibet, usually include eggplants.

Japan

In Japan the eggplant features largely in tempura, a delicate dish of fish and vegetable pieces dipped in a light batter and deep-fried until crisp and golden. In order to cook the eggplants as quickly as the other ingredients, the long, thin varieties are preferred over the round ones.

Above *Ping Tung Long is popular in Asian cooking.*

Below *A selection of eggplants grown under glass.*

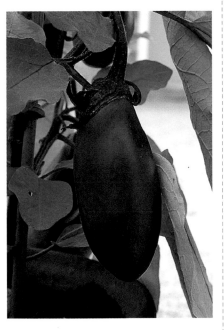

Left Apple Green, a 1997 trial variety of eggplant, with Turkish Orange, which looks more like a tomato.

Thai

Thai cooking often features eggplants, mostly using the long, thin, green varieties. These shapes are ideal for slicing or cutting into dice for salads. Another popular Thai variety is the pea eggplant, shaped as the name suggests and which are added to dishes whole. Pea eggplants look very attractive, but are often hard to find, except in specialist stores.

Italy

Rustic Italian cooking is full of eggplants, and many of the most famous dishes, such as Caponata (see page 40), are from Calabria in the south, known for robust and gutsy flavors. Long thin varieties are available in Italy as well as the more rounded ones, and they are interchangable in recipes, the shape being often of more importance for appearance rather than flavor.

India

Eggplants are used in the many different styles of Indian cooking, vegetarian and non-vegetarian. They are used extensively in main dishes, as well as in a wide variety of relishes and preserves. The ability of the eggplant to absorb flavors makes it a valuable ingredient in curries, and the appearance of dishes is often enhanced by adding chile and turmeric.

Above Short Tom, a small, dark-purple vegetable, suitable for a wide variety of dishes.

introduction

Turkey

For many eggplant lovers it is not until the delights of Turkish cooking are explored that the true glory of the vegetable is revealed. Without the eggplant, it would seem, there is no Turkish cuisine. Turkish dishes are full of the mystery of smoky eggplant flesh, blended with tomatoes and oils, and an inspired blend of spices. The Turkish style is a wonderful mixture of warm Mediterranean flavors, married with the spiciness of north Africa and the Middle East.

The History of the Eggplant

Both India and China claim to be the original home of the eggplant, although there are no records of it growing in the wild. However, it is most likely that China was the source, and there are references to eggplants in records of market gardening dating from 500 BC.

It was certainly popular throughout Asia long before it reached Europe in the Middle Ages. Like so many "new" foods it was regarded at first with suspicion in the West, and was even referred to as the *apple of Sodom*! It was also regarded at first as a decorative plant, rather than one to eat and enjoy. In fact, it took a long time for the eggplant to be accepted in the West.

Varieties

Eggplants belong to the same family as potatoes, as do tomatoes and bell peppers. This is the deadly nightshade family, which might explain why eggplants had a bad press at first. All members of this family contain a certain amount of toxins, and in eggplants they are present in the immature fruits, in the stems and leaves. It is interesting to note that fruits picked when they are unripe do not keep for longer than a few hours at peak condition.

Many eggplants grow quickly to over one pound in weight. These are regarded as large eggplants for the recipes, while a medium eggplant weighs about 12 ounces. Smaller varieties have more specific uses. Tiny finger eggplants, and the white egg-shaped ones, are excellent for relishes and preserves which require whole fruits. Thai eggplants – the long, thin variety – are best for Eastern-style cooking, especially if they are to be sliced and stir-fried with other vegetables.

Above The unusual Asian Bride variety is ideal for slicing..

I have geared this book mainly to the supermarket shopper, and the recipes therefore can all be made with the more common purple varieties. However, supermarkets are waking up to eggplant culture, and many are now stocking round fruits for stuffing, stripy ones for presentation, and the longer thin varieties which work well for Eastern cooking.

Salting

I am often asked whether it is necessary to salt eggplants before cooking, a technique used to extract any bitter juices from the flesh. In most cases it isn't, but I do salt eggplant slices to soften them for making a mold, or for a shell that is to be stuffed and baked. Salting is not necessary for frying or broiling, when I can safely say, having tried both ways, that it seems to make no difference at all to the outcome.

Above Turkish Orange eggplants are unusually juicy.

Left Bambino are about the size of cherries and may be boiled or roasted whole. They make wonderful additions to salads.

Buying and Storing

It is essential to buy eggplants when they are really fresh, with a dark, shiny, and blemish-free skin. With most varieties the darker the skin the better. In addition to sweetness of flavor, a fresh eggplant will have a much more tender skin. You should also check that the stem is fresh-looking, and not shriveled or bruised. Buy them as needed, but if you have to store them, they are best loosely wrapped in a plastic bag and kept in the salad drawer of the refrigerator.

Growing Eggplants

Eggplants make wonderful greenhouse plants, and I have grown them successfully without heat, although they do like humidity. Pinch out the tops when they reach 2 feet tall, to encourage them to bush, and use canes to support the plants, especially when the fruits appear.

They appear to need high temperatures to set, especially the more unusual varieties. Once the fruits have set and the flowers have faded, make sure that the flowers drop off, otherwise the fruits will be blemished. Feed generously once a week with a tomato fertilizer once the fruits have set. To encourage maximum growth, limit the number of fruits on each plant to between six and eight.

Above Display eggplants growing in a pit house at West Dean Gardens.

Natural Cooking Partners

As the eggplant absorbs other flavors so easily, there are some ingredients which are natural partners and will always produce a successful dish.

Tomatoes can be used in all forms, including passata, sun-dried tomatoes, and tomato paste. The color greatly enhances the appearance of eggplant dishes, while well-reduced tomato sauces also add richness.

Left Many varieties of eggplant make very attractive plants. This is the striped Rossa Bianca.

Below Japanese Pickling is a variety ideal for use in relishes and preserves.

Olive oils may be rich, green, and fruity, or fragrant and light. Many dishes begin by frying eggplants in oil, so always use a well-flavored, preferably extra virgin oil.

Meats with a certain amount of fat will not only flavor the dish, but also help to keep the eggplant moist. Stuffed eggplants are always successful when filled with a ground meat filling, such as pork, lamb, or beef, as the fat content in the meat will help to soften the shells. However, for poultry or vegetable fillings with less fat, it is necessary to add stock or water to the baking dish, to enable the shells to cook through.

introduction

13

Above *The flowers of the eggplant range through
pink and purple, and clearly show their close
relationship to the potato.*

Appetizers and Salads

Eggplant Humus

For all humus fans. This version uses eggplant in place of chick peas, but the tahini gives the dip the flavor that you would expect.

SERVES 6

- 1 large eggplant
- 3 scallions, roughly chopped
- 1 red chile, seeded and chopped
- Grated rind and juice of ½ lemon
- 2 garlic cloves, crushed
- Salt and freshly ground black pepper
- 3 Tbsp olive oil, plus extra for drizzling
- ½ cup tahini
- Paprika, to sprinkle

Preparation time: 30 minutes

❶ Cook the eggplant on a barbecue, under a broiler, or in a hot oven until the skin is wrinkled and blistered and the flesh is tender. Turn once or twice during cooking. Cover with a damp cloth and leave to cool for about 10 minutes, then peel off the skin.

❷ Roughly chop the eggplant, then mix it in a bowl with the remaining ingredients. Spoon the mixture into a small serving dish. Drizzle with a little extra olive oil and sprinkle with paprika. Serve with warmed pita bread, or vegetable sticks for dipping.

Eggplant and Cheese Pâté

A creamy pâté to serve with toast or crackers. Use heavy cream or low-fat cheese according to your conscience.

SERVES 6

- 1 large or 2 small eggplants
- 1 cup cream cheese
- 1 garlic clove, crushed
- 1 green chile, seeded and chopped
- 1 Tbsp tomato paste
- Salt and freshly ground black pepper
- Paprika, to sprinkle

Preparation time: 40 minutes

· Chilling time 30 minutes

❶ Cook the eggplant over a barbecue, under a broiler, or in a hot oven until the skin is wrinkled and blistered and the flesh is tender. Turn once or twice during cooking. Cover with a damp cloth and leave to cool for about 10 minutes, then peel off the skin.

❷ Blend the eggplant with the remaining ingredients in a blender. Season well, then turn into a serving bowl. Sprinkle with paprika. Chill for 30 minutes before serving.

Eggplant Pesto

A relatively low-in-fat pesto with a hint of smokiness from the eggplant. If fresh basil is unavailable, try mixing one teaspoon of dried basil into chopped fresh parsley instead.

SERVES 4

- 1 large eggplant
- 1 large handful of fresh basil leaves
- 2–3 garlic cloves, roughly chopped
- ½ cup pine nuts
- ¾ cup freshly grated Parmesan cheese
- 1 tsp coarse sea salt
- ¼ cup olive oil
- Freshly cooked pasta, to serve
- Parmesan shavings and basil sprigs, to garnish

Preparation time: 40 minutes

---

❶ Cook the eggplant over a barbecue, under a broiler, or in a hot oven until the skin is wrinkled and blistered and the flesh is tender. Turn once or twice during cooking. Cover with a damp cloth and leave to cool slightly for about 10 minutes, then peel off the skin.

❷ Blend all the remaining ingredients together in a blender or food processor, then add the eggplant and blend again. Season to taste. Serve tossed with freshly cooked pasta.

appetizers and salads

Eggplant, Fennel, and Walnut Salad

The slightly aniseed flavor of the fennel and the crunch of the nuts contrast well with the eggplant.

SERVES 6

- ¾ cup olive oil
- 1 fennel bulb, thinly sliced, feathery leaves reserved for garnish
- 1 small red onion, sliced
- ¾ cup walnut pieces
- Sea salt and freshly ground black pepper
- 1 large eggplant, cut into ½-inch pieces
- 1 Tbsp red wine vinegar
- 1 tomato, skinned, seeded and chopped
- 1 Tbsp torn fresh basil leaves
- Basil sprigs, to garnish

Preparation time: 15 minutes

Cooking time: 15 minutes

Cooling time: 30 minutes

---

❶ Heat 3 tablespoons of olive oil in a skillet and add the fennel and onion. Cook until just soft but not browned, about 5 to 8 minutes. Remove with a slotted spoon and place in a salad bowl.

❷ Add 2 tablespoons of oil to the skillet, then stir in the walnut pieces and fry them for about 2 minutes, until crisp and browned but not burnt. Remove the nuts from the pan with a slotted spoon and drain on paper towels. Place the nuts in a bowl, sprinkle with salt, and toss until well coated and cool.

❸ Add 4 tablespoons of oil to the skillet, then add the eggplant and fry over a moderate heat until tender and browned on all sides. Remove from the pan and add to the fennel and onion.

❹ Add the remaining oil to the skillet with the red wine vinegar and a little salt and pepper. Heat, stirring, until the dressing is simmering, then pour over the vegetables in the bowl. Toss lightly, then leave to cool for 10 to 15 minutes.

❺ When the salad is still just slightly warm, add the salted walnuts, chopped tomato, and basil. Leave until cold, then serve garnished with fennel leaves and basil sprigs.

appetizers and salads

Eggplant and Orange Cream

An unusual cream with a Spanish flavor, using a fragrant olive oil, sage and orange. It is excellent served with roast or smoked duck.

SERVES 4 TO 6

- 2 eggplants
- Grated rind and juice of 1 large orange
- 1 garlic clove, crushed
- 1 Tbsp chopped fresh sage
- Salt and freshly ground black pepper
- ¼ cup fragrant Spanish olive oil

Preparation time: 30 minutes

❶ Cook the eggplants over a barbecue, under a broiler, or in a hot oven until the skin is wrinkled and blistered and the flesh is tender. Turn once or twice while cooking. Cover with a damp cloth and leave for about 10 minutes to cool.

❷ Peel the eggplants, then chop the flesh roughly. Place in a blender or liquidizer with all the remaining ingredients and blend to a thick paste, seasoning well with salt and pepper.

❸ Serve as a dip, with vegetables or olive bread, or as a sauce with duckling, either hot or cold.

Eggplant Toasts

This is a variation on the ever-popular Chinese shrimp toasts. The eggplant can be shredded with a coarse grater, but you will find it easier to use a food processor.

SERVES 4

- 4 slices white bread, crusts removed
- Vegetable oil, for deep-frying
- Thinly sliced chiles and cilantro sprigs, to garnish
- Oyster sauce, to serve

EGGPLANT PASTE:

- ½ lb eggplant, peeled and shredded
- 1 egg white, lightly whisked
- 2 tsp sherry
- 2 tsp oyster sauce
- Pinch of ground ginger
- 2 tsp cornstarch
- Pinch of salt

Preparation time: 20 minutes
Cooking time: 10 minutes

❶ Mix the eggplant with the remaining paste ingredients. Cut the bread into bite-sized triangles, then spread on one side with the paste.

❷ Heat the oil to 320°F in a wok, then carefully add the triangles in batches with a spoon, paste side down, and fry for about 2 to 3 minutes, until the bread is golden brown. Remove with a slotted spoon and drain on paper towels. Keep warm until all the toasts are cooked.

❸ Serve warm with oyster sauce, garnished with sliced chiles and cilantro sprigs.

Eggplant Toasts

Minted Eggplant Salad with Yogurt

A creamy salad to serve with cold roast meat or poached salmon. I like to spice it up a bit with toasted cumin seeds, but fennel or coriander seeds work just as well.

SERVES 4 TO 6

- 1 Tbsp cumin seeds
- ½ cup fruity olive oil
- 1 large eggplant, sliced
- 1 garlic clove, crushed
- 2 Tbsp chopped fresh mint
- 1 cup plain yogurt
- Salt and freshly ground black pepper

Preparation time: 35 minutes

Cooling time: about 45 minutes

---

❶ Heat a large skillet over a moderate heat, then add the cumin seeds and dry-fry for 30 seconds or so, until fragrant and just starting to pop. Transfer to a saucer and leave until required.

❷ Heat the oil in the skillet, then add the eggplant slices and fry on both sides until lightly browned and tender. Do not be tempted to add more oil as some will run from the eggplant as it cooks. Remove the slices from the skillet with a slotted spoon and allow to cool a little, then place them in a shallow dish, sprinkle with the cumin, garlic, and mint and leave until cold.

❸ Spoon on the yogurt and season well, then toss together gently. Serve lightly chilled.

Thai Salad

Bright with the flavors of the Pacific, this is an exciting main course salad. Use ham in place of pork if you prefer, and mint instead of cilantro for a change.

SERVES 4

- 2 long, thin Thai or Japanese-style eggplants
- 2 hot Thai chiles, seeded if preferred, and finely sliced
- 2 shallots, finely sliced
- 2 Tbsp fish sauce
- Juice of two limes
- 1 Tbsp superfine sugar
- ½ cup finely chopped cooked pork
- 1 cup peeled shrimp, defrosted if frozen
- 2 Tbsp fresh whole cilantro leaves

Preparation time: 30 minutes

---

❶ Cook the eggplants over a barbecue, under a broiler, or in a hot oven until the skin is wrinkled and blistered and the flesh is tender. Turn once or twice while cooking. Cover with a damp cloth and leave for about 10 minutes to cool. Meanwhile, mix together the chiles, shallots, fish sauce, lime juice, and sugar in a bowl.

❷ Peel the eggplants and cut them into chunks. Toss the eggplants in the sauce, then add the pork and shrimp. Serve garnished with the cilantro leaves.

appetizers and salads

Cracked Wheat Salad

I love cracked wheat salads. The addition of eggplant, with its lovely purple-black skin, provides lots of color and texture.

SERVES 3 TO 4

- 1 cup cracked wheat
- 1½ cups finely diced cucumber
- 2 large tomatoes, seeded and chopped
- ½ cup olive oil
- 1 onion, finely sliced
- 1 eggplant, sliced, then slices halved
- 2 tsp ground cinnamon
- Salt and freshly ground black pepper
- 2 Tbsp raisins
- 1 Tbsp red wine vinegar
- 2 Tbsp chopped chives
- 2 tbsp chopped fresh parsley

Preparation time: 30 minutes
Cooking time: 15 minutes

---

❶ Place the cracked wheat in a bowl and just cover with cold water. Leave to stand for 20 to 30 minutes, until the wheat has absorbed all the water. Turn into a fine nylon strainer, and press out any surplus water with the back of a large spoon. Place in a large bowl and add the cucumber and tomato.

❷ Heat the oil in a skillet and add the onion, eggplant and cinnamon. Cook until browned on all sides, then remove from the skillet with a slotted spoon. Season the cracked wheat well, then add the raisins.

❸ Add the vinegar to any oil remaining in the pan, season lightly then pour over the wheat. Add the chives and parsley and mix well. Arrange the onion and eggplant on top of the salad before serving.

TIP

Cracked wheat, available from good health food stores, is the lightly crushed grain of wheat. It is sometimes called bulghar wheat, and is a nutritious staple in the Middle East. Delicious in salads and it also makes excellent pilaf - **see Eggplant and Cracked Wheat Pilaf on page 95.**

appetizers and salads

Eggplant Guacamole

For all diet-conscious lovers of Mexican food! This is a lower-calorie version of the traditional avocado dip.

SERVES 4 TO 6

- 1 large eggplant
- 1 avocado, peeled and chopped
- Grated rind and juice of 1 lime
- 2 tomatoes, seeded and chopped
- 1 green chile, seeded and finely chopped
- 1 Tbsp very finely chopped onion
- 1–2 garlic cloves, crushed
- Salt and freshly ground black pepper
- Olive oil, to drizzle
- Paprika, to sprinkle

Preparation time: 10 minutes

Cooking time: 40 minutes

❶ Preheat the oven to 425°F. Prick the eggplant all over, then place on a cookie sheet and roast for 30 to 40 minutes, until the skin is wrinkled and blistered, and the flesh is tender. Turn once or twice during cooking. Cover with a damp cloth and leave to cool completely.

❷ Peel the eggplant, then chop into small pieces. Blend to a fairly smooth paste in a blender or food processor, then turn into a small bowl. Toss the avocado in the lime juice, then add to the eggplant with the remaining ingredients. Stir carefully until well combined. Season generously with salt and pepper, then drizzle with a little olive oil and sprinkle with paprika.

❸ Serve in a small bowl with tortilla chips or warm toast.

Smoky Eggplant and Mint Dip

A refreshing salad to serve as a dip, or on a bed of salad leaves.

SERVES 4

- 2 large eggplants
- 2 tsp cumin seeds
- 1–2 garlic cloves, roughly chopped
- 2 Tbsp chopped fresh mint leaves
- Sea salt and freshly ground black pepper
- 1 cup thick plain yogurt
- 1 cucumber, finely diced

Preparation time: 10 minutes

Cooking time: about 30 minutes

❶ Cook the eggplants over a barbecue, under a broiler, or in a hot oven until until the skin is wrinkled and blistered and the flesh is tender. Turn once or twice during cooking. Cover with a damp cloth and leave to cool for about 10 minutes, then peel off the skin.

❷ While the eggplants are broiling, toast the cumin seeds in a dry skillet until just starting to pop, then transfer them to a mortar and allow to cool for a few minutes. Add the garlic, mint, and about ½ teaspoon of salt, then grind into a paste. Alternatively, crush with the end of a rolling pin.

❸ Chop the eggplant. Place in a blender with the cumin paste and blend into a thick purée. Add the yogurt and blend to a creamy paste. Turn into a bowl, stir in the cucumber and season to taste with salt and pepper.

Eggplant Guacamole

Ratatouille Niçoise

This is more a salad than a vegetable stew, with the ingredients cooked individually, but it has all the flavors of the classic Mediterranean dish.

SERVES 4 AS A MAIN COURSE, OR 8 AS AN APPETIZER

- About 7 Tbsp olive oil
- 1 large onion, chopped
- 2 garlic cloves, finely sliced
- 1 green bell pepper, cored, seeded, and sliced
- 1 zucchini, yellow if possible, sliced
- 1 long, thin eggplant, about 2 inches in diameter, cut into ¼-inch slices
- 2 cups canned chopped tomatoes
- ⅔ cup red wine
- 4–5 sprigs fresh thyme
- Salt and freshly ground black pepper
- 1 Tbsp torn fresh basil leaves
- ½ cup small black pitted olives
- 1⅓ cups diced feta cheese

Preparation time: 10 minutes
Cooking time: 30 minutes
Cooling time: 20–30 minutes

❶ Heat 3 tablespoons of olive oil in a large skillet, add the onion and cook over a medium heat until softened but not brown, about 5 minutes. Add the garlic and cook for a few seconds longer, then remove the onion and garlic with a slotted spoon and place in a large bowl.

❷ Add the green bell pepper to the skillet and cook slowly for 4 to 5 minutes, then remove with a slotted spoon and place in the bowl. Add 1 to 2 tablespoons more oil to the skillet, then add the zucchini and cook for 3 to 4 minutes, turning once.

❸ Remove the zucchini with a slotted spoon and add to the bowl. Add 1 to 2 more tablespoons of oil to the skillet, then add the eggplant slices and fry gently until lightly browned on both sides. It may be necessary to do this in batches. Remove the eggplant with a slotted spoon and add to the bowl.

❹ Add the tomatoes to the skillet with the red wine, thyme, salt, and pepper. Bring to a boil, then simmer gently for 5 minutes. Remove the thyme, then pour the hot sauce over the vegetables in the bowl. Leave to cool, tossing the vegetables in the sauce once or twice.

❺ Just before serving, add the torn basil leaves, olives and cheese. Serve at room temperature for the best flavor.

28

Eggplant à la Grecque

A marinated eggplant salad with mushrooms and chopped parsley. Serve with lots of bread to mop up the delicious juices.

SERVES 4 TO 6

- 1 large eggplant, sliced
- About ½ cup olive oil
- Salt and freshly ground black pepper
- 1–2 garlic cloves, crushed
- ½ lb mushrooms, sliced
- 2–3 Tbsp chopped fresh parsley

Preparation time: 25 minutes

Chilling time: 1–2 hours

---

❶ Preheat the broiler. Arrange the eggplant slices in the pan and brush with olive oil. Broil until browned, turning occasionally.

❷ Place the eggplant slices in a serving dish and add enough oil to moisten, but not so much that they are swimming in it. Season well, add the garlic, mushrooms and parsley and stir gently. Leave for 1 to 2 hours, then serve at room temperature for best flavor.

Eggplant Salad with Cranberries

I have used cranberries in this recipe, but you could just as well use pomegranate juice and seeds. The sweet tartness of the fruit complements the eggplant very well.

SERVES 4 TO 6

- 3 Tbsp mild, fragrant olive oil
- 1 eggplant, cut into ¼-inch dice
- 1 small onion, finely sliced
- ½ cup cranberry juice
- 1 garlic clove, crushed
- ⅓ cup dried cranberries
- Salt and freshly ground black pepper
- ⅔ cup toasted whole wheat bread crumbs
- Chopped fresh parsley, to garnish

Preparation time: 10 minutes

Cooking time: 15 minutes

Cooling time: 30 minutes

---

❶ Heat the oil in a skillet, add the eggplant and onion and cook over a moderate heat until the oil has all been absorbed. Add the cranberry juice and continue cooking until the eggplant is soft. Transfer to a serving bowl, add the garlic and allow to cool.

❷ Add the dried cranberries and season to taste. Stir in the toasted bread crumbs and sprinkle with parsley just before serving.

Eggplant with Ginger

An Asian salad to serve with any Chinese, Japanese, or Thai meal. The clean taste of ginger provides a perfect appetizer.

S ERVES 4

- 2 large eggplants
- 2-inch piece fresh ginger
- 2 Tbsp light soy sauce
- 2 Tbsp sesame oil
- 1 Tbsp torn fresh cilantro leaves
- Salt and sugar, to taste

Preparation time: 30–40 minutes

Marinating time: 15 minutes

---

❶ Cook the eggplants on a barbecue, under a broiler, or in a hot oven until the skin is wrinkled and blistered and the flesh is tender. Turn once or twice during cooking. Cover with a damp cloth and leave to cool for about 10 minutes, then peel off the skin. Cut the flesh into large pieces and place in a bowl.

❷ Grate the ginger coarsely, including the skin, then gather up the shreds in your hand, and squeeze the juice over the warm eggplant. Add all the remaining ingredients, stir well and leave for 10 to 15 minutes to marinate. Serve on a bed of lightly stir-fried bell pepper strips, or other Asian vegetables.

Eggplant and Lentil Salad

An excellent winter salad as an alternative to coleslaw – filling and tasty.

SERVES 4

- 3 Tbsp sesame seeds
- 5 Tbsp olive oil
- 1 large onion, finely chopped
- 1 tsp ground cumin
- 1–2 garlic cloves, crushed
- 1 large eggplant, diced
- ½ cup orange lentils
- 2 cups canned chopped tomatoes
- 1 cup vegetable or chicken broth
- Salt and freshly ground black pepper
- 1 Tbsp freshly chopped mint

Preparation time: 10 minutes

Cooking time: 35 minutes

❶ Heat a large pan over a medium heat, then add the sesame seeds and dry fry for 2 to 3 minutes, stirring constantly, until evenly toasted. Transfer onto a plate.

❷ Heat 3 tablespoons of the oil in the pan. Add the onion and cumin and cook until starting to brown, then add the garlic and eggplant and continue cooking for 2 to 3 minutes. Add the lentils, chopped tomatoes, broth and seasoning. Bring to a boil. Cover and simmer for 30 minutes. Season and leave to cool.

❸ Add the toasted sesame seeds and mint to the mixture, then stir in the remaining olive oil. Cool the salad for 30 minutes before serving. Do not serve too cold, or the full flavor will be lost.

Eggplant and Shrimp Fritters

I usually steer clear of dishes which need to be deep-fried, but these Italian-style fritters are so delicious that they make an exception to my rule.

SERVES 4

- 1 large eggplant, thickly sliced
- ⅔ cup peeled shrimp, finely chopped
- Vegetable oil, for deep-frying

BATTER:

- 3 large eggs
- 1 cup freshly grated Parmesan
- Salt and freshly ground black pepper
- Freshly grated nutmeg
- 3 Tbsp all-purpose flour
- 3 Tbsp white bread crumbs
- Lemon slices, halved, to garnish

Preparation time: 20 minutes

Cooking time: 30 minutes

❶ Add the eggplant slices to a large pan of boiling water and boil for 5 minutes. Drain and when cool enough squeeze the slices dry and mix them with the chopped shrimp.

❷ Separate 2 eggs, reserving the whites. Mix the yolks with the cheese, and season with salt, pepper, and nutmeg, then mix with the eggplant and shrimp.

❸ Shape into 12 walnut-sized balls. Add the remaining egg to the reserved egg whites and beat them together. Spread the flour and the bread crumbs on 2 plates. Coat the balls in the flour, dip them into the egg and then into the crumbs.

❹ Heat the oil in a deep-fryer to 375°F. Fry the fritters in batches until they are golden brown and crisp. Drain on paper towels. Serve either hot or cold, garnished with lemon slices.

Eggplant and Shrimp Fritters

Crispy Eggplant Slices

This is a good appetizer for an informal supper party as it can be prepared well in advance, and baked as your guests arrive.

SERVES 4

- Vegetable oil
- 2 large eggs, beaten
- 1 Tbsp milk
- ¾ cup whole wheat bread crumbs
- 2 Tbsp chopped fresh parsley
- ⅓ cup grated Parmesan cheese
- ⅓ cup pine nuts, finely ground
- ⅓ cup cornmeal or polenta
- Salt and freshly ground black pepper
- 1 eggplant, cut into ½-inch slices
- Salad leaves, to garnish

Preparation time: 20 minutes

Cooking time: 30 minutes

❶ Preheat the oven to 350°F and oil 2 cookie sheets. Beat the eggs and milk together in a shallow bowl. Mix all the other ingredients except the eggplant on a flat plate.

❷ Dip the eggplant slices first into the egg, then into the crumb mix, coating them thoroughly. Place in a single layer on the cookie sheets. Bake in the preheated oven for 30 minutes, or until the eggplant slices are tender and the crumbs are crisp. Serve garnished with salad leaves.

Eggplant Cream

Sometimes called Hünkâr Begendi or Sultan's Delight, this delicate creamy dish is served as a sauce for meat or fish, or as a dip with pita bread.

SERVES 6 TO 8

- 2 large eggplants
- 1 Tbsp lemon juice
- 4 Tbsp butter
- ⅓ cup all-purpose flour
- 2 cups milk
- Salt and freshly ground black pepper
- ¾ cup freshly grated Parmesan
- Chopped fresh parsley, to garnish
- Pitta bread, to serve

Preparation time: 20–40 minutes

Cooking time: 30 minutes

❶ Cook the eggplants under the broiler, or in a hot oven until the skins are wrinkled and blistered and the flesh is tender, turning once or twice. Cover with a damp cloth and leave to stand for about 10 minutes, then peel off the skin. Leave the eggplant flesh in a bowl of cold water with the lemon juice to prevent discoloration.

❷ Melt the butter in a large pan, then remove from the heat and stir in the flour. Cook slowly over a low heat for about 2 minutes, then put the pan to one side. Drain the eggplant and squeeze dry with your hands. Add to the pan and blend with a potato masher. Gradually stir in the milk.

❸ Bring the sauce slowly to a boil over a low heat, then season to taste. Simmer the sauce for about 15 minutes. Stir in the cheese, then season again if necessary. Pour into a warm bowl or dish and sprinkle with chopped parsley.

appetizers and salads

34

Eggplant Cream

Eggplant Caviar

Eggplant pastes have long been referred to as caviar. Nothing like the real thing, but the texture is slightly similar – a rough purée with a savory tang.

SERVES 4

- 2 eggplants
- Salt and freshly ground black pepper
- Walnut oil
- 2 large tomatoes, chopped
- 1 large garlic clove, chopped
- 6 scallions, chopped
- 1 Tbsp fresh chopped oregano
- 2 hard-cooked eggs, very finely chopped

Preparation time: 1 hour

Chilling time: 1 hour

❶ Preheat the oven to 425°F. Prick the eggplants all over, then place them on a cookie sheet and season lightly. Drizzle with a little walnut oil, then bake in the preheated oven for 30 to 40 minutes, or until tender. Leave to cool, then roughly chop the eggplants, including the skin.

❷ Purée the eggplants in a food processor with the tomatoes, garlic, and scallions and enough walnut oil to make a paste. Season well, then stir in the oregano and chopped eggs. Chill slightly, then serve with fresh hot toast.

Eggplant with Tomatoes and Mozzarella

A simple broiled dish to serve as a main course salad or an appetizer, with crusty bread to mop up the juices.

SERVES 4

- 2 large eggplants, cut lengthwise into ¼-inch slices
- Salt and freshly ground black pepper
- ⅓ cup olive oil
- Small handful of fresh basil leaves, roughly torn
- 8 small ripe tomatoes, halved
- 2 garlic cloves, finely sliced
- 4½ oz mozzarella, drained and thinly sliced
- 1 tsp balsamic vinegar

Preparation time: 40 minutes

Cooking time: 30 minutes

❶ Make a single layer of the eggplant slices on a cookie sheet and sprinkle generously with salt. Leave for at least 30 minutes, then rinse thoroughly under cold water and pat dry with paper towels.

❷ Pour the oil into a shallow dish. Dip each slice of eggplant into the oil, then cook the slices, a few at a time, in a griddle pan for 3 to 4 minutes on each side.

❸ Layer the eggplant in an ovenproof dish with the basil, tomatoes and garlic. Finish with a layer of eggplant, season well, then cover with the sliced mozzarella.

❹ Add the balsamic vinegar to the oil left in the griddle pan and pour it over the cheese. Broil under a moderate heat for 4 to 5 minutes, until the cheese is bubbling and starting to brown. Serve with mixed salad leaves and bread to mop up the juices.

Eggplant Sandwiches

This recipe uses slices of eggplant as the "bread" in baked ham and cheese sandwiches. They are delicious.

SERVES 4

- 1 large eggplant, cut lengthwise into eight ¼-inch slices
- Salt
- Olive oil, for brushing
- 2 slices ham, smoked turkey, or cooked chicken
- 2 slices Cheddar or other sharp cheese
- 1 large egg, beaten
- 1 Tbsp milk
- 1½ cups fresh white bread crumbs
- Salad leaves, to garnish

**Preparation time: 20 minutes
plus 30 minutes salting time
Cooking time: 20 minutes**

---

❶ Lay the eggplant slices on a cookie sheet in a single layer, then sprinkle salt over them and leave for 30 minutes. Rinse under cold water and pat dry on paper towels.

❷ Preheat the oven to 400°F. Brush the slices lightly with olive oil on the outsides, then assemble them into 4 sandwiches. Fill each one with half a slice of cheese and half a slice of ham, trimming them to fit so that the filling does not overflow.

❸ Dip the sandwiches into the egg, beaten with the milk, then into the bread crumbs. Press on sufficient bread crumbs to give a good coating.

❹ Place the sandwiches on an oiled cookie sheet and bake in the preheated oven for 20 minutes, or until lightly browned. Serve immediately with a salad garnish.

appetizers and salads

37

Spiced Eggplant Salad

This is based on a traditional north African recipe, where the eggplant is flavored with paprika, cumin and lemon juice.

SERVES 4 TO 6

- About 1 cup olive oil
- 2 eggplants, sliced
- 2 tsp sweet paprika
- 2 tsp ground cumin
- 2 garlic cloves, finely sliced
- ½ cup pistachio kernels
- Grated rind and juice of 1 lemon
- Salt and freshly ground black pepper
- Sugar, to taste

Preparation time: 10 minutes
Cooking time: 15 minutes

---

❶ Heat ½ cup of oil in a large skillet and add the eggplant, paprika, and cumin. Cook over a gentle heat so that the spices do not burn, adding more oil as necessary; the eggplant will take about 10 minutes to cook through. Add the garlic to the skillet halfway through the cooking.

❷ Transfer the eggplant to a serving bowl, then add the pistachios, lemon rind, and juice. Season well, adding a little sugar if you wish. Allow the salad to chill for about an hour before serving.

Spring Rolls

A variation on the popular Chinese dish, delicious dipped in soy sauce.

SERVES 4

- 3 Tbsp peanut oil, plus extra for brushing
- 1 eggplant, sliced
- 1 small onion, finely sliced
- 3 Tbsp oyster sauce
- ½ cup water
- 2 cups prepared stir-fry vegetables, defrosted if frozen
- Salt
- 8 sheets phyllo pastry, measuring about 7 x 12 inches
- Soy sauce

Preparation time: 1 hour
Cooking time: 15 minutes

---

❶ Heat the oil in a pan, add the eggplant and onion and cook gently. Mix the oyster sauce with the water, add to the pan and continue to cook slowly for about 10 minutes, until the eggplant is tender. Remove from the heat and leave until cool enough to handle.

❷ Preheat the oven to 400°F and lightly oil a cookie sheet. Mix the eggplant and onion with the stir-fry vegetables. Fold the phyllo sheets in half and brush with oil to keep them moist. Divide the vegetable mixture between them. Sprinkle each one with a few drops of soy sauce.

❸ Fold the bottom and sides of the pastry in over the filling, then roll the pastry up into a sausage, brushing the edges with a little oil. Place on the prepared cookie sheet and brush lightly with oil again.

❹ Bake the spring rolls in the preheated oven for 10 to 15 minutes, until the pastry is crisp. Serve immediately.

Spring Rolls

Caponata

The region of Calabria in southern Italy is famed for the pungency of its dishes, with the exciting flavors of simple ingredients skilfully blended together. Caponata is one of the most famous of all eggplant dishes and there are many supposedly authentic recipes for it. This is my personal favorite.

SERVES 4

- 2 large eggplants, cut into ½-inch chunks
- Salt
- ½ cup fruity olive oil
- 1½ cups mixed pickled vegetables, such as onions, gherkins, bell peppers, roughly chopped
- ⅓ cup capers
- 2 celery sticks, chopped fine
- ½ cup pitted green olives
- 1 Tbsp sugar
- ⅔ cup red wine vinegar
- 2 Tbsp pine nuts

Preparation time: 45 minutes

Cooking time: 30 minutes

---

❶ Layer the eggplants in a colander, sprinkling each layer with salt, then leave to stand for 30 minutes. Rinse thoroughly in cold water, then drain and pat dry on paper towels.

❷ Pour all but 2 tablespoons of the oil into a large skillet, add the eggplant and cook for 10 to 12 minutes, or until browned and soft.

❸ Pour the remaining oil into a small pan, add the pickles, capers, celery, and olives and cook slowly over a very low heat for about 10 minutes, until well softened. Add the sugar and vinegar and continue to cook slowly until the smell of the vinegar has gone.

❹ Drain the eggplants of any excess oil, then add to the other vegetables with the pine nuts. Add a little salt to season, if necessary. Serve the caponata warm or cold.

TIP

The best way to buy pitted green olives is loose at a good delicatessen. They keep well for a couple of weeks in the refrigerator. Aside from being available for your cooking, they make irresistible pre-dinner nibbles.

---

appetizers and salads

40

Barbecued Eggplant with Spicy Pepper Butter

An unusual appetizer to keep the folks happy while the meat is cooking on the barbecue. Serve with soft rolls or pita bread.

SERVES 4

• 2 eggplants

SPICY BUTTER:

• ¼ lb (1 stick) butter

• 1 tsp finely chopped onion

• 1 garlic clove, crushed

• ½ tsp paprika

• ½ tsp green peppercorns, crushed

• 1 Tbsp chopped fresh cilantro

• Salt and freshly ground black pepper

Preparation time: 10 minutes

Plus chilling time: 1 hour

Cooking time: 40 minutes

❶ To make the spicy butter, beat the butter in a bowl with a wooden spoon until soft, then add all the remaining seasonings with salt and pepper to taste. Shape the butter into a roll, then cover in plastic wrap and chill for 1 hour.

❷ Cook the eggplants on the barbecue until the skins are blistered and wrinkled, and the flesh is tender. Turn them over several times during cooking. Do not cook them too quickly or the skins will burst.

❸ Carefully remove the eggplants from the barbecue, then cut them in half lengthwise. Score the soft flesh into diamonds, then top with a generous knob of the spicy butter and allow it to melt into the flesh.

Italian Griddled Eggplant

An Italian-style salad of cooked eggplant slices marinated in oil and mint and finished with toasted pine nuts and Parmesan.

SERVES 4

• 1 large eggplant, thickly sliced

• Olive oil, for brushing

• ⅓ cup pine nuts, toasted

• 2 Tbsp chopped fresh parsley

• Grated rind of 1 lemon

• Parmesan cheese shavings

MARINADE:

• ½ cup olive oil

• 1 garlic clove, crushed

• 12 large basil leaves, roughly torn

• 1 Tbsp chopped fresh mint

• Salt and freshly ground black pepper

• 1 Tbsp balsamic vinegar

Preparation time: 20–25 minutes

Standing time: 1–2 hours

❶ Preheat the broiler or griddle pan until very hot, then add the eggplant slices. Brush generously with olive oil, then broil or griddle until browned, turning frequently.

❷ Mix together the ingredients for the marinade in a shallow dish. Add the eggplant slices and turn them in the mixture. Leave for 1 to 2 hours, then stir in the pine nuts. Serve at room temperature, sprinkled with the parsley, lemon rind, and Parmesan.

Italian Griddled Eggplant

Griddled Eggplant and Goat Cheese Salad

In this marinated salad the spiced eggplant slices are broiled and served hot with goat cheese. Do try a true goat cheese, it is so good. The real thing should be eaten at its freshest.

SERVES 4

- 1 eggplant, thinly sliced
- Olive oil, for frying
- 3½ oz soft goat cheese, sliced

MARINADE:

- 1½ tsp cumin seeds
- ½ tsp coarse sea salt
- ½ cup red wine
- 2 Tbsp olive oil
- 1 Tbsp red wine vinegar
- Salt and freshly ground black pepper
- 1 garlic clove, crushed
- 1 Tbsp chopped fresh mint
- 1 tsp sugar

Preparation time: 45 minutes

Cooking time: 20 minutes

❶ To make the marinade, heat a small skillet, then add the cumin seeds and dry fry them for 30 to 45 seconds, until fragrant and starting to brown. Turn the seeds into a mortar with the sea salt and pound them with a pestle until finely ground. Alternatively, crush with the end of a rolling pin.

❷ Transfer the spice mixture to a shallow dish and add the remaining marinade ingredients. Add the eggplant slices, turning to coat well, then leave for at least 30 minutes.

❸ Shake the eggplant slices dry, and reserve the marinade. Griddle the slices with a little oil in a griddle pan or skillet. Place in an ovenproof dish and top with the sliced cheese.

❹ Drizzle with the remaining marinade then broil under moderate heat until lightly browned. Serve with crusty bread and a juicy, tomato salad.

appetizers and salads

44

Red Mullet with Eggplant and Arugula Pesto

Crab-topped Eggplant Slices

Shrimp and Eggplant Turnovers

Eggplant and Tuna Risotto

Tuna and Eggplant Kabobs

Eggplant with Gingered Crab and Vanilla Pasta

Roast Monkfish with Eggplant and Wine Sauce

Eggplant and Cod Bake

Stuffed Trout with Pine Nuts

Trout with Eggplant and Cranberry Sauce

Braised Squid with Eggplant

Marinated Swordfish with Eggplant Ribbons

Stuffed Mussels

Deep-fried Fish with Eggplant Couscous

Almond-coated Fishcakes with Thai Salad

Mediterranean Fish Stew

Salmon and Eggplant Kedgeree

Skate with Blackened Eggplant Butter

Fish and Eggplant Pie

Red Mullet with Eggplant and Arugula Pesto

A light fish dish with very robust flavors. Red mullet has a meaty taste which balances the pesto very well.

Preparation time: 45 minutes

Cooking time: 20 minutes

❶ First prepare the pesto. Place all the ingredients in a blender or food processor and blend to a smooth sauce. Season to taste, then turn into a small bowl.

❷ Lay the eggplant slices in a single layer on a cookie sheet. Sprinkle with salt and leave for 30 minutes. Preheat the oven to 400°F. Rinse the eggplant well under cold water and dry on paper towels. Heat the oil in a griddle pan, add the eggplants and cook until browned on both sides. Remove and keep warm in the oven.

❸ Add more oil to the griddle if necessary. Add the mullet fillets, skin side down, and cook for 1 to 2 minutes. Transfer the fish to a buttered cookie sheet and cook in the oven for 5 to 6 minutes.

❹ To serve, arrange 2 eggplant slices on individual warmed serving plates, then place a mullet fillet on each. Spoon a little of the pesto onto the plates, then serve immediately.

SERVES 4

- 2 eggplants, cut lengthwise into ½-inch slices
- Salt
- 2–3 Tbsp olive oil
- 8 large red mullet fillets
- Butter, for greasing

PESTO:

- 1 cup mixed arugula and parsley leaves, about half and half
- ⅓ cup freshly grated Parmesan cheese
- ⅓ cup pine nuts
- 2 garlic cloves, crushed
- ½ cup olive oil
- Salt and freshly ground black pepper

fish dishes

Crab-topped Eggplant Slices

Crab and eggplant have very complementary flavors. A little crab meat goes a long way in this dish, so it's not expensive to make.

SERVES 4 AS AN APPETIZER,
2 AS A MAIN COURSE

- 1 eggplant, sliced lengthwise into 4
- Salt
- Olive oil, for frying
- ¾ cup fresh white bread crumbs
- ¼ cup pine nuts
- Salt and freshly ground black pepper
- ½ cup freshly grated Parmesan cheese
- 1 Tbsp chopped fresh parsley
- 1–2 Tbsp melted butter
- ¾ cup crab meat

Preparation time: 50 minutes

Cooking time: 15 minutes

❶ Sprinkle the eggplant slices lightly with salt, then leave them to drain in a colander for 30 minutes. Preheat the oven to 425°F.

❷ Rinse the eggplant thoroughly in cold water, then dry on paper towels. Heat 2 tablespoons of oil in a skillet and cook the slices for 3 to 4 minutes on each side, until just cooked. Transfer the eggplant to a cookie sheet.

❸ Mix all the remaining ingredients together, binding them with the melted butter. Spoon onto the eggplant slices, then bake in the hot oven for 15 minutes, until the crab topping is lightly browned. Serve immediately, garnished with fresh parsley.

Shrimp and Eggplant Turnovers

These delicious light turnovers make an ideal quick lunch, served with a salad.

SERVES 4

- Butter, for greasing
- 1 eggplant, cut into ½-inch pieces
- 1 red and 1 green bell pepper, cored, seeded and cut into ½-inch pieces
- 1 red onion, finely chopped
- 3–4 Tbsp mild, fragrant olive oil
- 2 cups cooked peeled shrimp
- 1 cup cooked diced potato
- 3 Tbsp freshly chopped parsley
- Salt and freshly ground black pepper
- Grated rind and juice of ½ lemon
- 12 oz prepared puff pastry
- Milk, for glazing

Preparation time: 15 minutes

Cooking time: 25 minutes

❶ Preheat the oven to 400°F and lightly butter a cookie sheet.

❷ Heat the oil in a skillet. Add the eggplant, bell peppers, and onion and cook until just softened, then mix with the shrimp, potato, and parsley. Season the mixture and mix in the lemon rind and juice.

❸ Roll out the pastry into a rectangle about 14 x 9 inches, then cut out 4 circles about 5 inches in diameter. Damp the edges of the circles, then place a quarter of the filling on half of each circle. Fold the pastry over, sealing the edges of the pastry together.

❹ Place the turnovers on the prepared cookie sheet and brush them with milk. Bake for 25 minutes, or until the pastry is golden. Serve hot or cold.

fish dishes

Eggplant and Tuna Risotto

Fresh tuna is an excellent ingredient in risotto, especially marinated in a mixture of lime and chile. The sweetness of eggplant balances the dish perfectly.

SERVES 4

- 1 or 2 tuna steaks, weighing about ½ lb in total, cut into 1-inch pieces.
- 2 eggplants, cut into ½-inch pieces
- Salt
- 3–4 Tbsp olive oil
- 1 onion, finely chopped
- 1½ cups arborio rice
- 5 cups well-flavored broth
- 1 Tbsp chopped fresh cilantro
- 1 Tbsp chopped fresh parsley
- Parmesan cheese shavings

MARINADE:

- Grated rind and juice of 1 lime
- 6 scallions, finely sliced
- 1 red chile, seeded and chopped
- Salt and freshly ground black pepper
- 3 Tbsp fruity olive oil

Preparation time: 40 minutes

Cooking time: 30 minutes

---

❶ Mix all the ingredients for the marinade together in a bowl, then add the tuna, turning the fish over in the mixture. Leave for 30 minutes. Salt layers of eggplants in a colander. Leave for 30 minutes then rinse and dry.

❷ Heat the oil in a large skillet. Add the onion and cook until softened, then add the eggplant and continue frying until it just starts to brown.

❸ Stir the rice into the pan juices. Add one-third of the broth to the pan. Bring to a boil, then simmer until nearly all the liquid has been absorbed, stirring frequently, then repeat with half the remaining broth.

❹ Drain the tuna, reserving the marinade, then place under a hot broiler for 3 to 4 minutes turning once or twice; it should be starting to brown on the outside but still slightly pink in the middle. Meanwhile, add the remaining broth and reserved marinade to the risotto and simmer as before until the liquid is absorbed.

❺ Add the tuna and any pan juices to the risotto, season to taste, then sprinkle with the chopped herbs and the Parmesan shavings.

Tuna and Eggplant Kabobs

Perfect fish kabobs for the garden or beach barbecue or to broil indoors out of season.

SERVES 4

- 1 lb 5 oz fresh tuna steaks, about 1 inch thick, cut into 1-inch cubes
- 1 long, thin, Japanese-style eggplant

MARINADE:

- Grated rind and juice of 1 lime
- 4 Tbsp olive oil
- 1 garlic clove, crushed
- 2 Tbsp chopped fresh oregano and parsley mixed
- Salt and freshly ground black pepper

Preparation time: 10 minutes

plus 1 hour marinating

Cooking time: 15 minutes

---

❶ Place the tuna in a glass bowl, then add all the marinade ingredients. Stir well and leave for at least 1 hour, stirring once or twice.

❷ Half cook the eggplant on the barbecue or under the broiler, until the skin is just starting to wrinkle. Cut into ½-inch thick slices.

❸ Soak the kabobs sticks to prevent them charring on the grill. Thread the tuna and eggplant on skewers, then brush with the remaining marinade.

❹ Cook over a moderate heat for 5 to 6 minutes on each side, either on the barbecue or under the broiler, basting at intervals with any remaining marinade. Serve with a rice salad.

Eggplant with Gingered Crab and Vanilla Pasta

A most unusual and utterly delicious dish inspired by my friend Philip Britten, the Michelin-star chef at the Capital Hotel in London's Knightsbridge. Use lobster in place of the crab if you wish.

SERVES 4

- 2-inch piece fresh ginger
- 1½ cups crab meat
- 2 cups strong white bread flour
- 2 large eggs
- A few drops natural vanilla extract
- 1 vanilla bean, split and seeds removed
- ⅓ cup fragrant olive oil
- 1 eggplant, finely sliced
- 1-inch piece fresh ginger, peeled and finely chopped
- 1 tomato, skinned, seeded and chopped
- Salt and white pepper

Preparation time: 20 minutes

Cooking time: 10 minutes

---

❶ Grate the larger piece of ginger, including the skin, with a coarse grater. Place the crab meat in a bowl. Gather up the shreds of ginger in your hand, then squeeze the juice over the crab. Leave the crab to marinate in the ginger juice.

❷ Prepare the pasta. Put the flour in a bowl and make a well in the center. Beat the eggs with the vanilla extract and seeds, then pour into the flour. Bind to a stiff dough, then knead thoroughly. Roll out very thinly, or pass the dough through a pasta machine, until thin enough to cut into spaghetti. Drape over a pole or the back of a chair on a cloth to dry until ready to cook.

❸ Bring a large pan of salted water to a boil. Meanwhile, heat the oil in a skillet. Add the eggplant and chopped ginger and cook gently until soft and lightly browned. Add the pasta to the boiling water and cook just until it floats to the top of the water again, 1 to 2 minutes. Drain the pasta well and shake it dry.

❹ Add the marinated crab and juice to the eggplant and heat for about 1 minute. Add the pasta, and toss the mixture together. Add the chopped tomato, and season just before serving.

Roast Monkfish with Eggplant and Wine Sauce

This sounds sophisticated, but is very quick to cook. Use sour cream or plain yogurt if you prefer in the sauce, but I find that ordinary cream reduces more successfully.

SERVES 3

- 1 monkfish tail, weighing about 1lb 5 oz, filleted
- 2 Tbsp olive oil
- Knob of butter, plus extra for greasing
- Salt and freshly ground black pepper
- 2 tsp whole grain mustard
- 4 scallions, sliced
- 1 small eggplant, finely sliced
- ½ cup dry white wine
- 2–3 Tbsp fish broth or water
- ⅔ cup heavy cream
- 3 Tbsp chopped chives
- Salt and freshly ground black pepper

Preparation time: 10 minutes

Cooking time: 25 minutes

---

❶ Preheat the oven to 425°F. Pull the papery skin away from the monkfish. Heat the oil and butter in a large skillet, then quickly fry the fillets on all sides. Place them on a buttered cookie sheet, then spread them with the mustard. Roast in the preheated oven for 15 minutes.

❷ Add the scallions and eggplant to the pan and cook quickly until the eggplant has absorbed the liquid. Add the wine and continue to cook until the eggplant slices are tender. Add the broth and cream, and simmer until the sauce has reduced and thickened. Add the chives and season to taste.

❸ Slice the monkfish fillets into thick medallions and arrange them on warmed serving plates. Spoon the sauce over the fish, and serve with sautéed potatoes and steamed green beans.

Eggplant and Cod Bake

A simple bake with the flavors of the Mediterranean. I like to serve this with a crisp green salad and crusty French bread to mop up the juices.

SERVES 4

- Butter
- Olive oil, for frying
- 1 eggplant, sliced
- 1 large onion, finely sliced
- 1 garlic clove, crushed
- 2 Tbsp capers
- ⅓ cup black pitted olives, Provençal if possible
- 2 cups canned chopped tomatoes
- 1 Tbsp chopped mixed fresh herbs, such as parsley, oregano, marjoram
- Salt and freshly ground black pepper
- Four 6-oz pieces of thick cod fillet, skinned

Preparation time: 25 minutes

Cooking time: 20 minutes

❶ Preheat the oven to 400°F. Butter an ovenproof serving dish

❷ Heat 2 to 3 tablespoons of oil in a large skillet and fry the eggplant slices gently until tender but not brown. Drain on paper towels. Add a little more oil to the pan if necessary, then add the onion and cook until softened and just starting to brown. Stir in the garlic, capers, and olives, then add the tomatoes, herbs, and seasoning to taste. Simmer the sauce for about 5 minutes, until it is slightly thickened and the onion is cooked.

❸ Pour the sauce into the prepared dish, then nestle the cod fillets into it. Cover the fish with the eggplant slices and dot with butter. Place the dish on a cookie sheet if it seems very full and likely to bubble over, then bake in the hot oven for 20 minutes, until the eggplant slices are browned. Serve immediately.

fish dishes

Stuffed Trout with Pine Nuts

A simple way of pan-frying trout stuffed with an eggplant paste for a light lunch or supper dish.

SERVES 4

- 1 large eggplant
- 2 scallions, chopped
- 1 garlic clove, crushed
- 1 Tbsp tomato paste
- Salt and freshly ground black pepper
- 1 Tbsp chopped fresh oregano or flat-leaf parsley
- 1 Tbsp fresh bread crumbs, if necessary
- 4 trout, weighing about 8 oz each, cleaned and scaled
- 3 Tbsp butter
- ½ cup pine nuts
- Chopped fresh parsley, to garnish

Preparation time: 40 minutes

Cooking time: 20 minutes

---

❶ Cook the eggplant on a barbecue, under a broiler, or in a hot oven until the skin is blistered and wrinkled and the flesh is tender, turning from time to time. Cover with a damp cloth and leave for about 10 minutes, then peel off the skin and roughly chop the flesh.

❷ Place the eggplant in a food processor with the scallions, garlic, tomato paste, and seasoning to taste. Blend to a paste, then fold in the chopped oregano. If the eggplant is very juicy you may need to add 1 tablespoon of fresh bread crumbs to thicken the paste into a stuffing.

❸ Season the trout lightly inside and out. Spoon the eggplant paste into the trout, holding them closed if necessary with wooden cocktail sticks.

❹ Heat the butter in a large skillet, then add the trout and cook over a moderate heat for 6 to 8 minutes on each side, according to size. Add the pine nuts to the skillet when the fish has had half the cooking time on the second side. Remove the trout to a plate and keep them warm, then continue to stir-fry the pine nuts in the pan juices until they are browned. Spoon the nuts and the juices over the trout and garnish with a little freshly chopped parsley.

Trout with Eggplant and Cranberry Sauce

Eggplant and cranberries present a wonderful, winning combination; the cranberries balance any oiliness from the eggplant or the fish.

SERVES 4

- 4 Tbsp butter
- 2 Tbsp olive oil
- 1 eggplant, cut into ¼-inch dice
- 4 rainbow or brown trout, weighing 9–10 oz each
- ⅓ cup dried cranberries
- 3 kaffir lime leaves, finely shredded
- 2–3 Tbsp sour cream
- Salt and freshly ground black pepper

Preparation time: 10 minutes

Cooking time: 20 minutes

❶ Heat 3 tablespoons of butter and 1 tablespoon of oil together in a large skillet, then add the eggplant. Cook for 3 to 4 minutes until lightly browned, then remove with a slotted spoon and keep warm in an ovenproof dish.

❷ Add the remaining butter and oil to the skillet, then add the trout and fry them gently for 5 to 6 minutes on each side. Transfer them to a plate and keep warm in the oven while finishing the sauce.

❸ Return the eggplant to the pan and add the cranberries with the shredded lime leaves. Cook for 1 to 2 minutes, then add the sour cream. Continue heating until the cream has melted, season to taste, then serve with the sauce spooned over the fish.

Braised Squid with Eggplant

Many people are discouraged from eating squid by the rubbery texture. But when braised, squid is meltingly tender, and lends itself especially well to Chinese cooking.

SERVES 3 TO 4

- 3 Tbsp vegetable oil
- 1 lb prepared squid, defrosted if frozen, cut into rings and tentacles chopped
- 1 eggplant, sliced
- 1 large green bell pepper, cored, seeded, and cut into large pieces
- 1 large red bell pepper, cored, seeded, and cut into large pieces
- 12 oz Bok choy, cut into thick slices
- 1 large onion, roughly chopped
- 2 Tbsp cornstarch
- 1 cup water
- ½ cup sherry
- ½ cup soy sauce

Preparation time: 10 minutes
Cooking time: 30 minutes
---

❶ Heat the oil in a wok, then add the squid and fry quickly for 1 to 2 minutes until it becomes opaque. Remove from the wok with a slotted spoon.

❷ Add the eggplant to the wok and cook until lightly browned, adding a little extra oil if necessary, then add the remaining vegetables. Blend the cornstarch with a little of the water, then add to the wok with the remaining water, sherry and soy sauce. Bring to the boil, stirring all the time, then return the squid to the wok and mix with the vegetables.

❸ Cover and simmer gently for 15 minutes. Serve immediately, with plain boiled rice or noodles.

Marinated Swordfish with Eggplant Ribbons

Swordfish readily absorbs the flavors of marinades, and I like to use lime for a really fresh tang. Ribbons of fried eggplant provide an unusual garnish.

SERVES 4

- 4 swordfish steaks, about ½ inch thick and weighing about 5 oz each
- 3 Tbsp olive oil
- 1 small, long eggplant, halved and sliced into fine ribbons

MARINADE:

- Grated rind and juice of 2 limes
- 3 Tbsp fruity olive oil
- 3 scallions, finely chopped
- Salt and freshly ground black pepper
- 1 garlic clove, crushed
- 1 Tbsp chopped fresh parsley

Preparation and marinating time: up to 4 hours

Cooking time: 10 minutes

❶ Mix all the ingredients for the marinade in a shallow dish, then add the swordfish. Leave to marinate for 1 to 4 hours, turning the steaks in the mixture once or twice.

❷ Heat the oil in a large skillet. Drain the swordfish, reserving the marinade, then fry it quickly in the hot oil, allowing 2 to 3 minutes on each side. Remove the fish from the skillet and keep it warm.

❸ Add the marinade to the skillet and heat it gently, then add the eggplant ribbons and cook quickly until they are soft and beginning to brown. Arrange the ribbons on the swordfish steaks before serving, spooning any remaining juices over the fish.

Stuffed Mussels

I first discovered the delights of stuffed mussels in Brussels, where they have restaurants that specialize in them. The easiest mussels for stuffing are the large, green-lipped variety. The ones I buy are from New Zealand, and very meaty.

SERVES 4

- 20 large green-lipped mussels, on the half shell
- 4 Tbsp olive oil
- 1 large onion, finely chopped
- 1 red chile, seeded and very finely chopped
- 1 small eggplant, very finely chopped
- 2 garlic cloves, crushed
- Salt and freshly ground black pepper
- ¾ cup fresh whole wheat bread crumbs
- Chopped fresh parsley, to garnish

Preparation time: 20 minutes

Cooking time: 15 minutes

---

❶ Preheat the oven to 425°F. Loosen the mussels on the half shells and arrange them on a cookie sheet.

❷ Heat the oil in a large skillet. Add the onion and chile and cook until starting to soften, then add the eggplant and garlic. Continue cooking for 5 to 6 minutes, until all the vegetables are soft and lightly browned. Season well, then add the bread crumbs and mix thoroughly.

❸ Pile a teaspoonful of filling into each shell over the mussel, then bake in the hot oven for 12 to 15 minutes, until piping hot. Serve immediately, garnished with chopped parsley.

fish dishes

59

Deep-fried Fish with Eggplant Couscous

You can use any firm, white fish fillets for this unusual recipe.

SERVES 4

- ¼ cup olive oil
- 1 eggplant, cut into ¼-inch dice
- 1 tsp ground turmeric
- ½ cucumber, cut into ¼-inch dice
- 6 scallions, finely chopped
- ⅓ cup pistachio nuts, roughly chopped
- ⅓ cup dried apricots, finely chopped
- 1½ cups well-flavored vegetable broth
- 1 cup couscous
- 1 tsp white wine vinegar (optional)
- Vegetable oil, for deep-frying
- 1 large egg white
- 2 Tbsp heavy cream
- 1 cup fine whole wheat flour
- 1 tsp chili powder
- 2 tsp ground cumin
- Salt and freshly ground black pepper
- 1 lb filleted white fish, cut into 1-inch pieces
- Lemon wedges, to garnish

Preparation time: 30 minutes
Cooking time: 10–20 minutes

❶ Heat the olive oil in a skillet. Add the eggplant and turmeric and fry for 3 to 4 minutes, until soft. Turn into a bowl and add the cucumber, scallions, nuts, and apricots.

❷ Bring the broth to a boil in a small pan, then add the couscous. Cover, remove from the heat and leave for 20 minutes.

❸ Heat the oil for deep-frying in a large pan to 375°F. Meanwhile, whisk the egg white in a bowl until just frothy, then stir in the cream. Mix the flour on a flat plate with the spices and a little salt and pepper. Toss the fish in the egg and cream, rubbing the mixture into the flesh. Coat the pieces in the seasoned flour.

❹ Deep-fry the fish in 2 to 3 batches for about 3 minutes, then remove with a slotted spoon and drain on paper towels. Keep the cooked fish warm.

❺ Stir the couscous into the vegetables and season well. Add a teaspoon of wine vinegar if you wish. Make a mound of couscous on each plate, then top with the deep-fried fish.

Almond-coated Fishcakes with Thai Salad

Don't be put off by the number of ingredients in this recipe; it is very straightforward and utterly delicious.

SERVES 4 AS A MAIN COURSE,
8 AS AN APPETIZER

- 2¾ cups fresh white bread crumbs
- 3–4 Tbsp milk
- 1 Tbsp peanut oil
- 4 scallions, finely sliced
- 1 lb white fish fillets, skinned and cut into ¼-inch dice
- 1 large egg, beaten
- 1–2 Tbsp chopped fresh cilantro
- 1 Tbsp chopped fresh parsley
- Salt and white pepper
- 2–3 Tbsp mayonnaise
- ½ cup ground almonds
- 2–3 Tbsp fragrant olive oil

SALAD:

- 2 long, thin Thai eggplants
- 1–2 hot Thai chiles, seeded if preferred, and finely sliced
- 4 scallions, finely sliced
- 2 Tbsp fish sauce
- Juice of 2 lemons
- ½ piece lemon grass, bruised and finely sliced
- 2 lime leaves, finely shredded – use dried if fresh are not available
- 2 Tbsp superfine sugar
- ¾ cup snow peas, finely shredded lengthways
- ¾ cup baby corn, finely shredded lengthways

Preparation and marinating time:
1 hour
Cooking time: 15 minutes

---

❶ First make the salad. Cook the eggplants on a barbecue, under a broiler or in a hot oven, until blackened and wrinkled, turning once or twice. Cover with a damp cloth and leave to cool for about 10 minutes, then peel off the skin. Chop the eggplant into large chunks, then add to all the other salad ingredients in a large bowl and leave to marinate for at least 30 minutes.

❷ Soak 2 cups of the bread crumbs in the milk for a few minutes, then squeeze them dry and discard the milk. Heat the peanut oil in a large skillet. Add the scallions and cook until soft but not browned. Remove with a slotted spoon and mix with the bread crumbs in a large bowl. Add the fish, egg, cilantro, and parsley. Season to taste, then add just enough mayonnaise to bind the mixture together.

❸ Mix together the remaining bread crumbs and the ground almonds on a flat plate. Shape the fish mixture into 8 large fishcakes, then coat with the almond bread crumbs, pressing the coating onto the fishcakes.

❹ Heat the olive oil in the skillet, then add the fishcakes and fry gently for 4 to 5 minutes on each side. Serve the fishcakes on a bed of the salad, with some of the salad juices spooned around.

Mediterranean Fish Stew

Making a large casserole of mixed seafood is an expensive business unless you have ready access to fishermen landing their catch on the quayside. Adding an eggplant to the pot makes the fish go much further, and gives a certain sweetness.

SERVES 4

- 4 Tbsp olive oil, plus extra for drizzling
- 1 large onion, chopped
- 1 large eggplant, cut into 1-inch cubes
- ½ lb prepared squid rings
- ½ cup dry white wine
- 2 cups canned chopped tomatoes
- 2¼ lb assorted white fish fillets, skinned and cut into pieces
- 2 cups well-flavored fish broth
- Salt and freshly ground black pepper
- 1 lb mussels, scrubbed and debearded
- Grated rind and juice of 1 lemon
- 2 Tbsp chopped fresh flat-leafed parsley
- Toasted French bread or ciabatta, to serve

Preparation time: 15 minutes

Cooking time: 20 minutes

---

❶ Heat the oil in a large deep pan. Add the onion and cook over a low heat for about 4 minutes until softened but not browned. Add the eggplant and squid and fry quickly until all the oil has been absorbed, then add the wine and tomatoes. Stir the fish into the pan, then add sufficient broth to just cover the fish.

Season with salt and pepper, then bring gently to a boil. Cover the pan and cook for 5 to 6 minutes, until the fish is just cooked but not breaking up.

❷ Add the mussels to the pan, return the stew to a boil, then cover and cook for a further 2 to 3 minutes, until all the shells have opened. Discard any that do not open.

❸ Add the lemon rind and juice, then season again if necessary and add the chopped parsley. Serve in deep bowls with slices of toasted bread, and a little extra olive oil drizzled over each serving.

Salmon and Eggplant Kedgeree

I love kedgeree, and have included eggplant and sultanas, and used fresh salmon to provide a good color contrast to the extra vegetables. Add a splash of cream before serving if you wish, and a spoonful of mango chutney for extra spice.

SERVES 4

- 1½ cups easy-cook long-grain rice
- Salt and freshly ground black pepper
- ½ lb salmon fillet, skinned
- 4 Tbsp butter
- 1 Tbsp curry paste
- 1 onion, sliced
- 1 eggplant, sliced
- ⅓ cup raisins
- 3 hard-cooked eggs, chopped

Preparation time: 20 minutes

Cooking time: 15 minutes

❶ Cook the rice in plenty of boiling, salted water for 10 to 12 minutes, until tender. Drain thoroughly in a colander.

❷ Poach the salmon fillet in a pan of barely simmering water for 4 to 5 minutes, until just cooked. Drain the salmon, allow to cool slightly, then flake, removing any bones.

❸ Melt the butter in a large skillet with the curry paste. Add the onion and eggplant and cook for about 5 minutes over low heat, until soft. Add a little extra butter if necessary to keep the vegetables moist. Keep the heat low so that the spices do not burn. Add the rice and salmon to the pan, mix carefully and cook gently for 2 minutes.

❹ Add the chopped eggs to the kedgeree with the raisins, then season to taste. Serve immediately.

Skate with Blackened Eggplant Butter

A variation on a traditional fish dish; the eggplant gives just a little more flavor. The delicious flesh of skate is firm and sweet. Use sole if you prefer.

SERVES 4

- 4 Tbsp butter
- 2 Tbsp olive oil
- 1 small eggplant, cut into ¼-inch dice
- 1 garlic clove, crushed
- 2 Tbsp capers
- 4 wings of skate, weighing about ½ lb each
- Salt and freshly ground black pepper
- 1 Tbsp chopped fresh parsley
- 2 Tbsp lemon juice

Preparation time: 5 minutes

Cooking time: 15 minutes

---

❶ Heat the butter and oil together in a large skillet, then add the eggplant and cook over a moderate heat for 4 to 5 minutes, until softened and starting to brown. Add the garlic and capers and cook for another minute. Remove the vegetables from the skillet with a slotted spoon, and keep warm.

❷ Add the skate to the skillet and cook for 3 to 4 minutes on each side, adding a little more butter only if absolutely necessary. Return the eggplant to the skillet just before the fish is ready, season well and add the parsley with the lemon juice.

❸ Serve the skate wings with the eggplant butter spooned over.

Fish and Eggplant Pie

This is called a fish pie, although there is no pastry or potato topping in sight! Instead, the topping is made of slices of griddled eggplant over a filling of mixed shellfish and fillets of flounder. It makes a wonderful summer dish.

SERVES 4

- 2 large eggplants, cut lengthwise into ¼-inch slices
- Salt and white pepper
- 3 Tbsp butter, plus extra for greasing
- 3 Tbsp all-purpose flour
- 2 cups milk
- ½ cup dry white wine
- 2 Tbsp chopped chives
- 2 cups mixed shelled shrimp and mussels, defrosted if frozen
- ½ lb flounder fillets, skinned and cut into 1-inch pieces
- 2–3 Tbsp olive oil
- Paprika, for sprinkling

Preparation time: 45 minutes

Cooking time: 25 minutes

---

❶ Arrange the eggplants in a single layer on a cookie sheet, then sprinkle them with salt and leave for 30 minutes. Rinse thoroughly in cold water, then pat dry on paper towels.

❷ Preheat the oven to 400°F. Melt the butter in a large pan over a moderate heat, then remove from the heat and stir in the flour. Cook gently for 1 minute, then gradually stir in the milk off the heat. Add the wine, then bring the sauce slowly to a boil. Season lightly and add the chives, then stir in the shellfish and flounder. Pour into a buttered ovenproof dish.

❸ Heat a griddle pan or skillet and add the olive oil. Cook the eggplant slices in batches until browned on both sides, adding more oil if necessary. Overlap the slices on top of the fish.

❹ Bake the pie in the preheated oven for 20 minutes. Sprinkle with a little paprika before serving with creamy potatoes and green vegetables.

Lamb and Eggplant Curry

Lamb and Eggplant Kabobs

Eggplant Stuffed with Lamb and Couscous

Beef, Eggplant, and Bell Pepper Soup

Meatballs with Eggplant and Tomato Sauce

Eggplant Goulash

Eggplant Stuffed with Lamb and Egg

Eggplant and Turkey Burgers

Potted Ham with Eggplant

Spiced Pork and Eggplant Chop Suey

Eggplant Stuffed with Pork and Mushroom

Beef and Eggplant Biriani

Beef with Dates and Eggplant

Rich Eggplant Râgout

Braised Chicken with Eggplant and Prunes

Chicken Moussaka

Roast Chicken with Eggplant Paste

Deep-fried Eggplant and Chicken Strips

Chicken and Eggplant Risotto

Venison Sausage and Eggplant Casserole

Meat and Poultry Dishes

Lamb and Eggplant Curry

Lamb and eggplants both readily absorb spices and seasonings, and are therefore perfect for curries. Try the parathas on page 120 as an additional accompaniment.

SERVES 6

- ½ cup vegetable oil or ghee
- 2 eggplants, finely sliced
- 1 lb boneless shoulder or leg of lamb, diced
- ⅓ cup creamed coconut, crumbled or chopped
- Roughly torn cilantro leaves, to garnish

CURRY PASTE:

- 2 large onions, roughly chopped
- 4 garlic cloves, roughly chopped
- 2 green chiles, seeded and chopped
- 2-inch piece fresh ginger, peeled and roughly chopped
- 1 Tbsp curry paste or powder
- 2 tsp salt
- 2 Tbsp tomato paste

Preparation time: 15 minutes

Cooking time: 1½ hours

❶ Blend together all the ingredients for the paste in a blender.

❷ Heat the oil in a large pan, then add the eggplant slices and cook over a medium heat for 8 to10 minutes, until softened and starting to brown. Add the prepared curry paste and cook for 2 to 3 minutes, then stir in the diced lamb. Cook for 3 to 4 minutes over a moderately high heat, until the meat is starting to brown, then add the coconut. Cover the pan and cook slowly for 1 hour, stirring from time to time and adding a little water, if necessary, to prevent the curry from sticking.

❸ Season to taste with salt, then garnish with cilantro leaves and serve immediately, with boiled rice or parathas (page 120).

TIP

Side dishes of cucumber sliced in to plain yogurt, or chopped celery and red bell pepper, served in small bowls or ramekins make attractive accompaniments to spiced dishes.

meat and poultry dishes

Lamb and Eggplant Kabobs

The rich juices of the lamb help to moisten and flavor the eggplant in these delicious kabobs. Serve with rice if you prefer, but they make ideal party or barbecue food when served in warm pita bread.

SERVES 4 TO 6

- 1 lb boned leg or shoulder of lamb, cut into 1-inch cubes
- 1 large eggplant, cut into 1-inch cubes
- Salt
- 12 cherry tomatoes

MARINADE:

- Grated rind and juice of 1 lemon
- Grated rind and juice of 1 lime
- 1 Tbsp chopped fresh cilantro
- 1 hot red chile, very finely chopped
- Salt and freshly ground black pepper
- 2 Tbsp olive oil

DRESSING:

- ⅔ cup sour cream
- ⅔ cup plain yogurt
- 3 Tbsp snipped chives
- 1 Tbsp chopped fresh parsley

Preparation time: 1¼ hours

Cooking time: 15 minutes

---

❶ Place the lamb in a shallow dish. Mix all the ingredients for the marinade together, then pour the mixture over the lamb. Leave to marinate for at least 1 hour.

❷ Place the eggplant in a colander and sprinkle with salt. Leave for at least 30 minutes, then rinse with cold water. Pat dry on paper towels.

❸ Mix all the ingredients for the dressing together, then spoon into a small serving bowl.

❹ Drain the lamb, reserving the marinade, and thread onto 12 kabob skewers with the eggplant and tomatoes. Do not pack the pieces too closely together. Cook the kabobs on a barbecue or under a broiler for 12 to 15 minutes, turning occasionally and basting with the reserved marinade, until the lamb and eggplant are browned and tender.

❺ Serve on the skewers or in warmed pita breads, with a spoonful of the dressing.

Eggplant Stuffed with Lamb and Couscous

A filling baked eggplant recipe that only needs a salad to accompany it. Couscous is easy to cook and makes an excellent stuffing for vegetables.

SERVES 4

- 2 eggplants
- Salt and freshly ground black pepper
- 1¼ cups well-flavored broth
- Good pinch of saffron
- 1 cup couscous
- 6 green cardamoms, lightly crushed and seeds removed
- 1 tsp ground ginger
- 2 garlic cloves
- 3 Tbsp olive oil, plus extra if necessary
- 1 large onion, finely chopped
- ½ lb lamb, finely sliced
- 1 green chile, seeded and chopped
- ½ cup ready-to eat dried apricots, finely chopped
- Butter, for greasing

Preparation time: 40 minutes

Cooking time: 40 minutes

---

❶ Cut the eggplants in half lengthways, leaving the stalks to help keep the eggplants in shape during cooking. Cut and scoop out the flesh, leaving a shell about ¼-inch thick. Salt the shells lightly, then leave them for 30 minutes upside down on paper towels to drain. Chop the flesh.

❷ Bring the broth to a boil with the saffron, then pour in the couscous. Cover the pan, remove from the heat and leave to stand.

❸ Grind the cardamom seeds, ground ginger, and garlic to a rough paste in a pestle and mortar, or with the end of a rolling pin. Preheat the oven to 425°F.

❹ Heat the oil in a pan, add the onion and spice paste, and cook over a low heat until soft. Add the lamb, chile, and eggplant flesh, and cook quickly until the lamb has browned, adding a little extra oil if necessary. Stir in the couscous and chopped apricots. Season to taste.

❺ Rinse the eggplant shells thoroughly in cold water, then place in a buttered aluminum ovenproof dish. Pile the filling into the shells, then cover with buttered aluminum foil and bake in the preheated oven for 20 minutes. Remove the foil and cook for a further 10 to 15 minutes, until the top is browned. Serve with a mixed, tossed salad.

meat and poultry dishes

Beef, Eggplant, and Bell Pepper Soup

A spicy broth or soup with the flavors of the Pacific Rim. I serve this as a lunch or supper dish with bread, but you could add a spoonful of cooked rice to each helping to make it more substantial.

SERVES 4 TO 6

- ¼ lb boneless chuck steak
- 3 Tbsp peanut oil
- 1 large onion, finely chopped
- 1 small eggplant, cut into ¼-inch dice
- 1 hot red chile, seeded and very finely chopped
- 1 green bell pepper, cored, seeded, and chopped
- 1-inch piece fresh ginger, peeled and finely sliced
- 1 stick lemon grass, bruised and finely chopped
- 3 fresh lime leaves, finely shredded (use dried if fresh are unavailable)
- 5 cups well-flavored broth
- Soy sauce and salt, to taste

Preparation time: 15 minutes

Cooking time: 1 hour

❶ Cut the beef into ½-inch strips, then slice it very finely. Heat the oil in a large pan, then add the beef and cook quickly until well browned. Add the onion, eggplant, chile, bell pepper, ginger, and lemon grass, then cover the pan and cook slowly for 4 to 5 minutes.

❷ Add the lime leaves and broth, then bring to a boil. Cover and simmer for at least 1 hour, until all the ingredients are tender and the flavors have blended.

❸ Season to taste with soy sauce and salt before serving.

Meatballs with Eggplant and Tomato Sauce

Meatballs make a welcome change to the more usual ground beef sauce for pasta.
Simmer the meatballs gently to prevent them breaking up during cooking.

SERVES 4

MEATBALLS:

- 1 lb ground lamb
- 6 scallions, finely chopped
- 1¼ cups fresh whole wheat bread crumbs
- 1 Tbsp tomato paste
- ½ tsp ground turmeric
- Salt and freshly ground black pepper
- 1 large egg, beaten
- Grated Parmesan cheese, to serve (optional)

SAUCE:

- 3 Tbsp olive oil
- 1 eggplant, cut into ½-inch chunks
- 1 onion, finely diced
- 1 garlic clove, finely sliced
- ½ tsp ground turmeric
- 1 tsp ground cumin
- 4 cups canned chopped tomatoes
- 1 bay leaf
- Salt and freshly ground black pepper
- 8–10 fresh basil leaves, torn

Preparation time: 25 minutes
Cooking time: 30 minutes
---

❶ Mix all the ingredients for the meatballs together. Shape the mixture with wet hands into walnut-sized balls.

❷ To make the sauce, heat the oil in a large skillet, then add the eggplant and fry gently until lightly golden. Add the meatballs, together with the onion, garlic, turmeric, and cumin, and cook until the meatballs are browned all over. Add extra oil only if the meatballs are sticking.

❸ Add the tomatoes and bay leaf with salt and pepper, and bring the mixture to a boil. Simmer gently for 20 minutes, then season to taste. Add the basil just before serving.

❹ Serve with pasta, sprinkling a little grated Parmesan over the meatballs if wished.

Eggplant Goulash

Perhaps this isn't a true goulash, but paprika works well with eggplant.

SERVES 4 TO 6

- 3 Tbsp olive oil
- 1 large onion, finely chopped
- 1 Tbsp caraway seeds
- 1½ lb boneless shoulder or leg of pork, cut into 1-inch pieces
- 2 Tbsp sweet paprika
- 1 green and 1 red bell pepper, cored, seeded, and cut into 1½-inch pieces
- 1 eggplant, cut into 1½-inch pieces
- 2 garlic cloves, finely sliced
- 2 cups canned chopped tomatoes
- 2½ cups well-flavored broth
- Salt and freshly ground black pepper

Preparation time: 25 minutes
Cooking time: 2 hours
---

❶ Preheat the oven to 325°F. Heat the oil in a pan, then cook the onion and caraway seeds slowly for 5 to 6 minutes over a low heat, until the onions are soft but not browned. Dust the pork with the paprika, then add to the pan and cook over a slightly higher heat until the pork has browned. Do not cook too quickly or the paprika will burn.

❷ Add the bell peppers, eggplant, and garlic, and continue cooking slowly for about 2 minutes, until the vegetables are just starting to soften, then add the tomatoes and broth. Season well with salt and pepper, then cover the casserole and cook in the preheated oven for 2 hours.

❸ Season the casserole to taste and serve with boiled rice or noodles.

Eggplant Stuffed with Lamb and Egg

A delicious and unusual light lunch or supper dish. Serve with boiled rice, pilaf, or saffron-flavored couscous.

SERVES 4

- 2 eggplants
- Salt and freshly ground black pepper
- 2 Tbsp olive oil
- 1 large onion, finely chopped
- 1 lb ground lamb
- 2 tsp ground cumin
- 1 tsp pumpkin pie spice
- 2 garlic cloves, crushed
- 1 Tbsp tomato paste
- 2 hard-cooked eggs, roughly chopped
- 2 Tbsp capers, rinsed
- Butter, for greasing

Preparation time: 40 minutes
Cooking time: 20 minutes
---

❶ Preheat the oven to 425°F. Cut the eggplants in half lengthways through the stalks. Scoop out the flesh, leaving a shell about ¼-inch thick. Salt the eggplants, then leave them to drain upside down for 30 minutes. Roughly chop the flesh.

❷ Heat the oil in a pan, add the onion and cook gently until soft. Add the lamb, cumin, pumpkin pie spice, and garlic and cook until the lamb has browned. Stir in the tomato paste, then cover and cook for 10 minutes. Add the egg and capers, then season the filling well. Rinse the shells, then pat them dry.

❸ Place the shells in a buttered oven-proof dish, then fill with the lamb and egg mixture. Cover the dish with foil, then bake for 20 minutes.

Eggplant and Turkey Burgers

My husband thought there ought to be a burger recipe in this book, so here it is! I have tried to conjure up the flavors of Italy, using dolcelatte in the burgers and ciabatta rolls to hold them. Don't fry the eggplant slices in too much oil, so that they are very juicy, or the burgers will become soft and very difficult to eat.

SERVES 4

- 4 ciabatta rolls
- 14 oz lean, boned turkey or chicken, cut into strips
- 4 scallions, roughly chopped
- ½ cup crumbled dolcelatte or other blue-veined cheese
- 4 halves sun-dried tomatoes, roughly chopped
- 2 garlic cloves
- Salt and freshly ground black pepper
- Olive oil, for frying
- 4 large, thick eggplant slices
- Lettuce leaves
- Mustard or mayonnaise, for serving

Preparation time: 15 minutes

Cooking time: 10 minutes

❶ Warm the rolls in a low oven. Process the turkey, scallions, cheese, tomatoes, and garlic to a paste in a food processor, in 2 batches if necessary. Season the mixture, then shape into 4 flat burgers.

❷ Heat 1 to 2 tablespoons of olive oil in a large skillet and add the burgers and eggplant slices. Fry gently for 4 to 5 minutes on each side, adding extra oil only if the burgers are sticking.

❸ Split the warm rolls and place a slice of eggplant in the bottom of each. Top with a burger, some lettuce, and a dollop of mayonnaise or mustard. Cover with the top of the roll, then enjoy!

Potted Ham with Eggplant

A rich mousse, set in individual molds lined with eggplant slices. Serve with lots of salad and fresh toast.

SERVES 4

- 2 large eggplants
- Salt and freshly ground black pepper
- ⅔ cup milk
- 1 Tbsp butter
- 1 Tbsp all-purpose flour
- 2 tsp Dijon or pepper mustard
- Olive oil, for frying and greasing
- 4 Tbsp dry white wine
- 1 tsp powdered gelatin
- 1 cup cooked chopped ham
- ⅔ cup heavy cream
- 2 Tbsp chopped fresh parsley

Preparation time: 1½ hours

Cooking time: 2 hours

---

❶ Slice one eggplant very thinly. Lay the slices on a cookie sheet in a single layer, sprinkle with salt, then leave for 30 minutes. Cook the other eggplant over a barbecue, under a broiler, or in a hot oven until the skin is wrinkled and blistered and the flesh is tender; turn once or twice during cooking. Cover with a damp cloth and leave for about 10 minutes, then peel off the skin.

❷ Heat the milk, butter, and flour together in a pan until thickened and boiling, stirring all the time. Add the mustard, salt and pepper, then remove from the heat, cover with waxed paper to prevent a skin forming, and leave until cold.

❸ Rinse the salted eggplant thoroughly and pat dry on paper towels. Heat a skillet or griddle pan, add a little oil, then cook the slices on both sides, a few at a time, until tender, adding more oil as necessary. Drain on paper towels and leave to cool.

❹ Heat the wine in a small pan until bubbling, then remove from the heat and sprinkle on the gelatin. Stir to dissolve, then leave for 2 to 3 minutes. Oil 4 individual bowls and line them with the eggplant slices, overlapping them slightly around the sides.

❺ Cut the peeled eggplant into chunks, then purée it with the ham in a blender or food processor. Whip the cream until thick and floppy. Mix the cream and the ham mixture into the sauce, blending well. Season with pepper; the ham should provide all the salt required. Stir the gelatin again, then fold it into the ham cream with half the parsley.

❻ Carefully spoon the ham into the prepared molds, banging them on the worktop to shake the mixture down. Chill for at least 2 hours before turning out the molds onto individual plates. Sprinkle with the remaining parsley and serve with toast and salad.

Spiced Pork and Eggplant Chop Suey

A spiced, Chinese-style dish of marinated pork and crispy, stir-fried vegetables. Make up your own vegetable mix, or use prepared stir-fry vegetables from the supermarket if you are in a hurry. Serve with boiled rice or thread egg noodles.

SERVES 4

- 1 pork tenderloin, weighing about 1 lb
- 1½ lb mixed stir-fry vegetables, such as celery, carrot, bell peppers, snow peas, beansprouts
- 1 eggplant, halved lengthwise and sliced thinly
- 4 Tbsp peanut oil

MARINADE:

- 2-inch piece fresh ginger, roughly grated
- 1–2 garlic cloves, crushed
- 1 Tbsp five-spice powder
- 1 green chile, seeded and very finely chopped
- 4 Tbsp soy sauce
- 1 Tbsp chili sauce
- 1 Tbsp light brown sugar

Preparation and marinating time: 1¼ hours

Cooking time: 10 minutes

❶ Trim the pork and cut it into very thin slices. Squeeze the juice from the grated root ginger and mix it with the other marinade ingredients, then add the pork and toss the slices in the mixture. Leave to stand for at least 1 hour, turning occasionally.

❷ Meanwhile, prepare the vegetables for the stir-fry, cutting them all into thin 2-inch lengths.

❸ Heat the oil in a wok or a large skillet until almost smoking, then add the pork and eggplant. Stir-fry until both are well browned, about 4 minutes, then add the remaining vegetables. Continue to cook for a further 2 to 3 minutes, adding any remaining marinade. Serve immediately.

Eggplant Stuffed with Pork and Mushroom

Use small purple or striped eggplants for this dish, if available. I like to make a fresh tomato sauce to serve with it, making full use of the hot oven while it is on to bake the eggplants.

SERVES 4

- 4 small eggplants, round ones if possible, or 2 larger ones
- Salt
- 4 Tbsp olive oil
- 1 large onion, finely chopped
- 4 rashers unsmoked back bacon, chopped
- 1 garlic clove, crushed
- ½ lb ground pork
- 1 tsp paprika
- ¼ lb mushrooms
- Salt and freshly ground black pepper
- 1 Tbsp tomato paste
- 8–12 basil leaves, roughly torn
- Broth, wine or water
- Chopped fresh basil, to garnish

SAUCE:

- 8 ripe tomatoes, halved
- 1 small onion, quartered
- 2 garlic cloves, peeled but left whole
- 1 Tbsp light brown sugar
- Olive oil, to drizzle

Preparation time: 30 minutes

Cooking time: 40 minutes

❶ Preheat the oven to 450°F. Cut off the tops of the eggplants, if using round ones, and scoop out the flesh, leaving a shell about ¼ inch thick. If using oval eggplants, halve them, and scoop out the flesh. Salt lightly, then leave the shells for about 20 minutes upside down on paper towels to drain. Chop the flesh fine.

❷ Heat the oil in a pan. Add the onion and cook over a low heat with the bacon and garlic for about 5 minutes, then add the ground pork and paprika. Cook quickly until browned, then add half the eggplant flesh and mushrooms and cook for a further 2 to 3 minutes.

❸ Season the mixture, adding the tomato paste and basil. Add a little broth, wine, or water, if necessary, to moisten the mixture, then leave to simmer gently. Rinse the eggplant shells thoroughly in cold water and drain. Pack the filling into them, then place in a buttered ovenproof dish. Cover with aluminum foil.

❹ Arrange the sauce ingredients in a single layer in a roasting pan with the remaining eggplant flesh. Season well, adding the sugar and a drizzle of olive oil. Cook the sauce at the top of the oven with the eggplants underneath for 35 to 40 minutes, until the tomatoes have started to blacken.

❺ Remove the sauce ingredients from the oven and allow to cool slightly. Remove the foil from the eggplants and return to the oven until the sauce is completed. Tip all the roasted vegetables and their juices into a blender and process until smooth. Press the purée through a sieve with the back of a spoon to give a smooth sauce, then season to taste. Serve the stuffed eggplants with the tomato sauce, sprinkled with the chopped basil.

Beef and Eggplant Biriani

A wonderful spicy dish for lazy entertaining. Most of it can be prepared in advance and heated through at the last moment. For special occasions decorate with gold or silver leaf just before serving.

SERVES 6

- 6 Tbsp ghee or sunflower oil
- 1 lb chuck steak, cut into 1-inch pieces, or 1 lb cooked diced beef
- 2 bay leaves
- 2 cups Basmati rice, rinsed
- 2 large onions, finely sliced
- 1 tsp curry paste
- ⅓ cup sultanas
- ⅓ cup creamed coconut, finely chopped

CURRY SAUCE:

- 2 onions, roughly chopped
- 3 garlic cloves, roughly chopped
- 1 green chile, seeded and chopped
- 1 Tbsp mild curry paste
- 2 Tbsp tomato paste
- 1 Tbsp light brown sugar
- ⅓ cup ghee or sunflower oil
- 1 large eggplant, cut into ½-inch dice
- 1¼ cups light cream
- Salt
- 2–3 Tbsp chopped fresh cilantro

GARNISHES:

- 2 hard-cooked eggs, quartered
- ⅓ cup whole blanched almonds, fried until golden brown
- 2–3 tomatoes, sliced

Preparation time: 2½ hours

Cooking time: 30 minutes

❶ Preheat the oven to 325°F. Heat 3 tablespoons of the ghee or oil in a flameproof casserole, brown the meat, then add enough water to cover. Add the bay leaves, then bring just to a boil. Cover the casserole and cook in the preheated oven for approximately 2 hours.

❷ Rinse the rice then bring to a boil in a large pan of cold water. Stir, then cover and cook for 10 minutes. Drain and rinse thoroughly, then drain again.

❸ Prepare the curry sauce. Blend the onions, garlic, and chile with the curry paste, tomato paste, and sugar in a blender or food processor. Heat the oil in a large skillet, add the eggplant and cook until starting to brown, then add the curry sauce and continue to fry gently for 4 to 5 minutes. Stir in the cream and bring almost to a gentle simmer, then add salt to taste. Remove from the heat, and set aside ready to reheat at the last moment.

❹ Heat the remaining ghee or oil in a large skillet or wok, add the onions and cook until golden. Remove half with a slotted spoon, to use as garnish. Add the curry paste to the onions and cook for a further minute, then add 3 tablespoons of juices from the meat, or water, and cook for 1 minute longer.

❺ Drain the meat and add it to the pan, or add the leftover cooked meat if using. Stir-fry until it is well heated through and has absorbed the juices. Once hot, add the cooked rice to the pan with the chopped coconut and stir gently until piping hot. Reheat the sauce gently and add the cilantro.

❻ Serve the biriani decorated with the prepared garnishes, with the curry sauce spooned over.

Beef with Dates and Eggplant

This is my interpretation of a tagine, the stew from North Africa which is always sweetened either with dates, figs, prunes, or apricots, or with sugar or honey.

SERVES 6

- 5–6 Tbsp olive oil
- 6 pieces of chuck steak, each weighing about ½ lb
- 2 large onions, sliced
- 2 garlic cloves, finely sliced
- 2 tsp ground cumin
- 1 tsp ground turmeric
- 1 large cinnamon stick
- 6 cloves
- 2 cups canned chopped tomatoes
- Salt and freshly ground black pepper
- 1 cup dried pitted dates
- 1½ cups well-flavored broth
- 1 large eggplant, cut into thin slices

Preparation and salting time:
1 hour
Cooking time: 3½ hours

❶ Preheat the oven to 325°F. Heat 4 tablespoons of oil in a large flameproof casserole, then add the beef and fry quickly on both sides until browned. Remove with a slotted spoon and leave on a plate.

❷ Add a little extra oil to the casserole if necessary, then add the onions, garlic, and spices and cook until soft but not browned. Stir in the tomatoes, then season with salt and pepper and add the dates. Bury the meat back in the pan amongst the vegetables, then add sufficient broth to cover the meat. Bring gently to a boil, then cover the casserole and cook in the preheated oven for 2 to 2½ hours, until the beef is tender.

❸ Meanwhile, layer the eggplant slices in a colander, salting them well, then leave for 45 minutes. Rinse the slices thoroughly in cold water and pat them dry on absorbent paper towels.

❹ When the meat is tender, season the casserole to taste, then arrange the eggplant slices over the top and brush them liberally with olive oil. Raise the oven temperature to 350°F then bake the casserole, uncovered, for a further 30 to 40 minutes, until the eggplant slices are browned. Serve with cucumber and yogurt salad.

84

Rich Eggplant Râgout

There are spaghetti sauces, and then there are rich, flavorsome râgouts. I use a mixture of meats for this sauce, and add eggplant for extra richness. Serve with spaghetti, tagliatelle, or any flat pasta.

SERVES 6 TO 8

- 4 Tbsp olive oil
- 1 large onion, finely chopped
- 1 eggplant, cut into ½-inch chunks
- 1¼ cups ground beef
- 1¼ cups ground pork
- ½ lb chicken livers, finely chopped
- ⅔ cup red wine
- 4 cups canned chopped tomatoes
- 1 Tbsp tomato paste
- 2 garlic cloves, finely sliced
- 2–3 bay leaves
- Salt and freshly ground black pepper
- Freshly grated nutmeg, to taste

Preparation time: 25 minutes

Cooking time: 2 hours
---

❶ Heat half the olive oil in a large pan. Add the onion and cook for 4 to 5 minutes over a low heat until soft and transparent. Add the remaining oil and the eggplant, then cook quickly until the eggplant starts to brown. Stir in the meat and chicken livers, and continue cooking over a medium high heat until all the meat is browned.

❷ Pour the wine into the pan and continue cooking over a high heat until the wine has almost evaporated, stirring all the time to scrape up any sediment from the bottom of the pan. Lower the heat, then add all the remaining ingredients. Bring to a boil, then cook for at least 1 hour at a very slow simmer. If preferred, cover the pan and cook in a slow oven at 325°F.

❸ Season the râgout to taste. Serve as a pasta sauce with spaghetti or tagliatelle, use as a sauce for lasagne, or top with creamy potatoes mashed with olive oil and garlic for a baked pie with a difference!

Braised Chicken with Eggplant and Prunes

A most unusual casserole with a refreshing tang of lemon. I sometimes add ground cumin and ginger to the chicken when frying, but I really think the flavor relies on the brandy, lemon juice, and bay.

SERVES 4
- 2 eggplants
- 3 Tbsp olive oil
- 4 chicken pieces
- 1 large onion, finely sliced
- 2 large carrots, thickly sliced
- ⅔ cup brandy
- Grated rind and juice of 2 lemons
- ⅔ cup pitted prunes
- Salt and freshly ground black pepper
- 2 large bay leaves
- 1¼ cups chicken broth
- Sugar
- Chopped fresh parsley, to garnish

Preparation time: 40 minutes

Cooking time: 1 hour
---

❶ Preheat the oven to 325°F. Cook the eggplants over a barbecue, under a broiler, or in a hot oven until the skins have wrinkled and blistered and the flesh is tender. Turn once or twice during cooking. Cover with a damp cloth and leave for about 10 minutes to cool, then peel off the skin and roughly chop the eggplant flesh.

❷ Meanwhile, heat the oil in a flameproof casserole and quickly brown the chicken pieces on all sides. Add the onion and carrots and continue cooking for 3 to 4 minutes over a low heat. Heat the brandy in a large metal ladle until it ignites, then pour over the chicken, off the heat, and leave until the flames subside.

❸ Add the lemon rind to the chicken with the eggplant, prunes, and seasonings, then add just enough broth to cover the chicken. Bring the casserole to a boil, then cover and cook in the preheated oven for 1 hour, or until the chicken is tender and cooked through.

❹ Remove the bay leaves from the casserole, add the lemon juice, then season the chicken to taste, adding a little sugar if necessary. Garnish the casserole with chopped parsley just before serving. Creamy mashed potatoes would make an ideal accompaniment to the rich sauce.

meat and poultry dishes

Chicken Moussaka

Moussaka is one of the classic eggplant dishes, and I think that this is the best moussaka recipe that I have ever tasted! I use a covered pan to start the sauce as I find that less oil is required if the onion is half steamed in its own juices.

SERVES 4 TO 6

- ½ cup olive oil
- 2 large onions, chopped
- 1 lb boneless chicken, finely diced or chopped in the food processor
- 1–2 garlic cloves, crushed
- ⅔ cup red wine
- 2 cups canned chopped tomatoes
- 2 Tbsp freshly chopped oregano, plus extra for garnish
- Salt and freshly ground black pepper
- 1 Tbsp tomato paste
- 2 large eggplants, sliced
- Butter, for greasing

TOPPING

- 1 cup ricotta cheese
- ½ cup soft goat cheese with garlic and herbs
- ⅔ cup plain yogurt

Preparation time: 1 hour

Cooking time: 30 minutes

---

❶ Heat 2 tablespoons of the oil in a pan, add the onions, cover and cook gently until soft. Remove the lid and stir in the chicken with the garlic. Cook quickly until the chicken changes color. Add the wine, and cook until it has reduced by half. Add all the other ingredients, then simmer slowly for 30 to 40 minutes, until rich and thick.

❷ Preheat the oven to 425°F. Add 3 to 4 tablespoons of the oil to a skillet. Fry the eggplant slices a few at a time until browned on both sides, adding more oil as necessary. Remove with a slotted spoon and drain on paper towels.

❸ Layer the chicken sauce and eggplant slices in a buttered, oven-proof dish, finishing with a layer of eggplant. Blend the cheeses and yogurt together into a sauce, add salt and pepper to taste, and spoon the mixture over the eggplants. Bake for 25 to 30 minutes. Serve sprinkled with chopped oregano.

meat and poultry dishes

87

Roast Chicken with Eggplant Paste

A smoky eggplant paste forced under the skin of a chicken before roasting helps to keep it moist. A little ground turmeric adds extra color and spice.

SERVES 4 TO 6

- 1 eggplant
- Salt and freshly ground black pepper
- 2 carrots, cut into chunks
- 1 onion, cut in wedges
- 2 large zucchini, cut into chunks
- 1 green bell pepper, cored, seeded, and cut into large pieces
- 1 garlic clove, halved
- Olive oil, for drizzling
- 1 chicken, about 3½ lb
- Pinch of ground turmeric

Preparation time: 40 minutes

Cooking time: 1½ hours

---

❶ Cook the eggplant over a barbecue, under a very hot broiler, or in a hot oven until the skin is wrinkled and blistered and the flesh is tender. Turn once or twice during cooking. Cover with a damp cloth and leave for about 10 minutes, until cool enough to handle. Peel off the skin, then mash the flesh with salt and pepper to a smooth paste.

❷ Meanwhile, preheat the oven to 400°F. Place the vegetables and garlic in a roasting pan. Season them lightly and drizzle with olive oil. Carefully loosen the skin on the chicken breast and spread the breast with the eggplant paste, pushing it underneath the skin. Pat the skin back into position. Season the chicken well and sprinkle with a pinch of turmeric. Place the chicken on top of the vegetables.

❸ Roast in the preheated oven for 1 hour, or until the juices run clear when you insert a skewer into the thigh. Remove the chicken, wrap it in foil and leave to stand for 20 minutes before carving. Meanwhile, return the vegetables to the oven to continue roasting for 20 minutes.

❹ Carve the chicken, or cut it into portions, and serve together with the roasted vegetables.

meat and poultry dishes

Deep-fried Eggplant and Chicken Strips

A good supper dish to serve with a fine dollop of tartare sauce or mayonnaise and accompanied with an excitingly dressed mixed green salad.

SERVES 4

- 1 egg white
- 1 Tbsp heavy cream
- Vegetable oil, for deep-frying
- 1 large eggplant, cut into thin strips
- 2 large chicken breasts, cut into thin strips
- 3 Tbsp sesame seeds
- Salt
- Sliced lemon and mayonnaise, to serve

SPICED FLOUR:

- ½ cup fine whole wheat flour
- 2 tsp ground cinnamon
- 2 tsp paprika
- 1 tsp salt

Preparation time: 25 minutes

Cooking time: 15 minutes

❶ Mix the flour with the spices and salt in a shallow dish. Beat the egg white until just frothy, then mix it with the cream.

❷ Heat the oil for deep-frying to 375°F in a large pan. Dip the eggplant and chicken strips in the cream mixture, then turn them in the seasoned flour to coat well.

❸ Deep-fry the eggplant and chicken in batches until golden, then remove with a slotted spoon and drain on paper towels. Scatter with sesame seeds and salt, and serve with sliced lemon and mayonnaise.

Chicken and Eggplant Risotto

I love risottos and this one has all my favorite ingredients: moist chicken, smoky, mysterious eggplant, and fragrant saffron. A good risotto should be moist and the rice should still have a little bite in the middle. I serve the eggplant as a sauce on top of the risotto, and it works very well indeed.

SERVES 4

• 1 large eggplant
• 1 Tbsp lemon juice
• Good pinch of saffron strands
• 5 cups well-flavored chicken broth
• 3 Tbsp olive oil
• 1 large onion, finely chopped
• 2–3 celery sticks, finely sliced
• 2 chicken breast fillets, finely diced
• 2 garlic cloves, finely sliced
• 1½ cups arborio rice
• 2 Tbsp fresh flat-leaf parsley
• Salt and freshly ground black pepper
• 1 Tbsp fresh tomato paste or ketchup, optional
• ⅔ cup dry white wine
• 2–3 tomatoes, skinned, seeded and chopped

Preparation time: 30 minutes
Cooking time: 40 minutes

---

❶ Cook the eggplant over a barbecue, under a moderate broiler, or in a hot oven until the skin is wrinkled and blistered and the flesh is tender. Turn once or twice during cooking. Cover with a damp cloth and leave for about 10 minutes to cool slightly, then peel off the skin. Plunge the flesh into a bowl of water with a tablespoon of lemon juice, to prevent discoloration, and leave until required. Soak the saffron strands in the hot broth.

❷ Heat the olive oil in a large skillet over a moderate heat, add the onion and celery and cook until soft but not browned, then add the chicken. Cook over a slightly higher heat until the chicken is white all over, then add the garlic and the rice, tossing them in the skillet juices.

❸ Add about one-third of the broth to the skillet, then bring to a boil, and simmer, stirring frequently, until all the broth has been absorbed. Add half the remaining broth and repeat the simmering.

❹ Drain the eggplant and squeeze with your hands, extracting as much liquid as possible, then chop the flesh roughly and blend it with the parsley and seasonings to a smooth paste. Add a tablespoon of tomato paste or ketchup for color.

❺ Stir the wine into the risotto, then add the remaining broth and continue cooking until it has a creamy consistency. Add the chopped tomatoes just before the risotto is ready, and season to taste with salt and pepper.

❻ Serve on warmed plates, topped with a spoonful of the smoky eggplant paste.

meat and poultry dishes

90

Venison Sausage and Eggplant Casserole

I like to use venison sausages for this casserole, but if these are not available you can use any herby or spicy sausages.

SERVES 4

- 2 Tbsp olive oil
- 8 thick venison sausages
- 2 slices smoked bacon, diced
- 1 large onion, finely chopped
- 1 carrot, diced
- 1–2 garlic cloves, sliced
- ⅔ cup red wine
- 1 large eggplant, cut into ½-inch chunks
- 2 cups canned chopped tomatoes
- ½ cup French lentils
- 1 Tbsp tomato paste
- 1¼ cups beef broth
- Salt and freshly ground black pepper

Preparation time: 15 minutes

Cooking time: 1 hour

---

❶ Preheat the oven to 350°F. Heat the oil in a flameproof casserole, then add the sausages and cook them briefly until browned all over. Add the bacon, onion, carrot, and garlic, then cover the casserole and cook slowly for 4 to 5 minutes.

❷ Add the red wine, then cook rapidly until it is well reduced. Add all the remaining ingredients, then bring to a boil. Cover and cook in the preheated oven for 1 hour.

❸ Season, and serve from the pot.

meat and poultry dishes

Vegetable Dishes

93

Eggplant and Peppers, Szechuan-style

Szechuan cooking is very spicy. You could serve this as a main course by itself, with boiled or fried rice as an accompaniment, or with a meat or fish dish.

Serves 3 to 4

- Peanut oil, for frying
- 1 large eggplant, cut into 1-inch chunks
- 2 garlic cloves, crushed
- 2-inch piece fresh ginger, peeled and very finely chopped
- 1 onion, roughly chopped
- 2 green bell peppers, cored, seeded, and cut into 1-inch pieces
- 1 red bell pepper, cored, seeded, and cut into 1-inch pieces
- 1 hot red chile, seeded and finely shredded
- ½ cup well-flavored vegetable broth
- 1 Tbsp sugar
- 1 tsp rice or white wine vinegar
- Salt and freshly ground black pepper
- 1 tsp cornstarch
- 1 Tbsp light soy sauce
- Sesame oil, for sprinkling

Preparation time: 10 minutes

Cooking time: 15 minutes

---

❶ Heat 3 tablespoons of oil in a wok. Add the eggplant and stir-fry for 4 to 5 minutes, until lightly browned. Add more oil if necessary. Remove the eggplant with a slotted spoon and keep warm.

❷ Add a little more oil to the wok, then add the garlic and ginger, and fry for just a few seconds before adding the onions and bell peppers with the chile. Stir-fry for 2 to 3 minutes, then return the eggplant to the wok. Mix the remaining ingredients together and add to the wok.

❸ Continue to stir-fry until the sauce has boiled and thickened. Check the seasoning, adding a little more salt or soy sauce as necessary, then serve immediately, sprinkled with sesame oil.

vegetable dishes

94

Eggplant and Cracked Wheat Pilaf

I love to cook with cracked wheat as it retains a grainy texture and a nutty flavor. Use whatever vegetables you have to hand, but I find the combination of eggplant, fennel and peppers works very well indeed.

Serves 4

- 2–3 Tbsp olive oil
- 1 large onion, chopped
- 1 fennel bulb, trimmed and sliced
- 1 eggplant, cut into large dice
- 1 green bell pepper, cored, seeded, and chopped
- 1½ cups cracked wheat or bulgar wheat
- 2 cups canned chopped tomatoes
- 3 cups well-flavored broth
- Salt and freshly ground black pepper

Preparation time: 15 minutes

Cooking time: 20 minutes

❶ Heat the oil in a large skillet, add the onion and fennel and cook until just starting to soften. Stir in the eggplant and bell pepper, then cook for a minute or so before adding the wheat. Add the tomatoes and broth, then bring the pilaf to a boil.

❷ Simmer for 15 to 20 minutes, until the broth has been absorbed. Season well with salt and pepper, then serve with a crisp green salad.

vegetable dishes

95

Eggplant and Kidney Bean Chili

Eggplants make a good alternative to lentils for a vegetable-based chili sauce. The spicing in this is quite strong; use a little less chili powder if you prefer. Serve with brown rice or tortilla chips, and an avocado dip.

SERVES 4

- 3 Tbsp peanut oil
- 1 large onion, chopped
- 2 tsp chili powder
- 1 tsp ground cumin
- 1 large eggplant, cut into ½-inch chunks
- 1–2 garlic cloves, crushed
- 1 large cinnamon stick
- 2 bay leaves
- 3 cups puréed tomatoes or thick tomato juice
- Salt and freshly ground black pepper
- 2 cups canned red kidney beans and juice
- Boiled rice, to serve
- Sour cream and fresh cilantro leaves, to garnish

Preparation time: 10 minutes

Cooking time: 40 minutes

---

❶ Heat the oil in a large pan. Add the onion with the chili powder and cumin and cook for 4 to 5 minutes over a low heat, until the onion is soft but not browned. It is important to cook the onion slowly so that the spices do not burn.

❷ Add the eggplant and garlic, and cook for 1 to 2 minutes, then add the cinnamon and bay leaves with the puréed tomatoes or tomato juice. Add salt and pepper, then bring to a boil. Cover the pan and simmer the sauce slowly for 10 minutes, then add the kidney beans and their juice. Continue cooking for a further 10 minutes, then remove the cinnamon and bay leaves.

❸ Season the chili to taste, then serve on a bed of rice with a large spoonful of sour cream, garnished with cilantro.

Eggplant and Almond Rissoles

Rissole is a very old-fashioned word, but I love these little patties with a side salad and tartare sauce, or even tomato ketchup.

SERVES 4

- 1 large eggplant
- ⅔ cup milk
- 1 Tbsp butter
- 1 heaped Tbsp fine whole wheat flour, plus extra for flouring
- Salt and freshly ground black pepper
- 4 scallions, finely chopped
- 1 Tbsp chopped fresh oregano
- ½ cup ground almonds
- 1⅓ cups fresh whole wheat bread crumbs
- ½ cup olive oil
- 2 eggs, beaten
- 1 cup dry whole wheat bread crumbs, toasted – you will need more if you make your own toasted crumbs
- Tartare sauce and salad, to serve

Preparation time: 1 hour

Cooking time: 15 minutes
---

❶ Cook the eggplant on a barbecue, under a broiler, or in a hot oven until the skin is wrinkled and blistered and the flesh is tender, turning once or twice. Cover with a damp cloth and leave for about 10 minutes, then peel off the skin and chop the flesh roughly.

❷ Heat the milk, butter and flour together, stirring all the time, until thickened and boiling. Cook for 1 to 2 minutes, then season to taste and turn into a large bowl. Mix the eggplant with the scallions and oregano, then add to the sauce. Add the almonds, more seasoning, and bread crumbs to give a thick paste. Shape into 8 rissoles, flouring your hands as necessary.

❸ Heat the oil in a large skillet. Dip each rissole in the beaten egg and then in the toasted bread crumbs, pressing on the crumbs. Add the rissoles to the skillet and fry gently for 4 to 5 minutes on each side. Serve immediately with tartare sauce and salad.

Eggplant Olives with Nuts and Cheese

This makes a colorful vegetarian dish. If you are cooking it for friends and don't want any last-minute bother, it can be prepared well in advance and kept in the refrigerator until needed

SERVES 4

- 1 large eggplant, cut lengthwise into 8 slices
- Salt and freshly ground black pepper
- Olive oil, for frying
- 1 large onion, roughly chopped
- 1 small handful of fresh parsley
- 1 cup walnut pieces
- ¼ lb mushrooms, roughly chopped
- 1 cup whole wheat bread crumbs
- Butter, for greasing
- 2 cups canned chopped tomatoes
- ¾ cup grated Cheddar cheese

Preparation and salting time: 1 hour

Cooking time: 40 minutes

---

❶ Arrange the eggplant slices in a single layer on a cookie sheet, then sprinkle liberally with salt and leave to stand for at least 30 minutes. Rinse well under cold water, then pat dry on paper towels.

❷ Preheat the oven to 375°F. Heat 2 to 3 tablespoons of olive oil in a large skillet. Add the eggplant slices and fry on both sides until just soft. Remove from the skillet and lay on a plate.

❸ Place the onions, parsley, nuts, and mushrooms in a food processor and process until chopped very fine. Heat 1 to 2 more tablespoons of oil in the skillet, then add the onion mixture and fry gently for 2 to 3 minutes. Stir in the bread crumbs and season well.

❹ Place a little of the nut mixture on each slice of eggplant, then roll up and secure with wooden cocktail sticks. Place in a buttered ovenproof dish, then season lightly. Pour the chopped tomatoes over the eggplant olives, then scatter the grated cheese over them.

❺ Bake in the preheated oven for 40 minutes, until the cheese is browned and the eggplants are tender.

vegetable dishes

98

Mixed Vegetable Gumbo

Gumbo is a traditional dish of okra and spices from the southern states of America. It usually contains chicken or fish, but make it with just a good selection of vegetables for vegetarian friends.

SERVES 4

- ⅔ cup olive oil, plus extra if needed
- 2 large onions, chopped
- 1 red and 1 green bell pepper, cored, seeded, and cut into ½-inch squares
- 1 hot chile, seeded and finely sliced
- 2 garlic cloves, finely sliced
- 1 lb okra, cut into ½-inch slices
- 2 cups canned chopped tomatoes
- 2 Tbsp butter
- 3 Tbsp flour
- 2 tsp chili powder
- 1 tsp ground cumin
- 3½ cups vegetable broth
- 4–5 sprigs fresh thyme
- Salt and freshly ground black pepper
- 1 eggplant, cut into 1-inch pieces
- 1 long, thin eggplant, sliced
- Boiled rice, to serve (optional)

Preparation time: 40 minutes

Cooking time: 1 hour

❶ Heat 3 tablespoons of oil in a large pan. Add the onion and cook gently until softened but not browned. Add the peppers, chili powder, garlic, and okra. Cook for 5 minutes over a very low heat, then add the tomatoes. Cover and simmer for 15 minutes.

❷ Meanwhile, melt the butter in a large flameproof casserole, then add the flour and spices and cook over a low heat until bubbling gently. Remove from the heat and gradually add the broth, then the thyme. Return to the heat and bring slowly to a boil. Simmer the sauce for 1 to 2 minutes; it should be quite thin, even after boiling. Season well, then add the vegetable mixture. Cover and cook slowly for 30 minutes.

Eggplant with Garlic and Tomatoes

A quick and simple dish to cook when time is short.

SERVES 2

- 1 eggplant, sliced
- 1 large onion, sliced
- 1–2 tsp paprika
- ⅓ cup olive oil
- 4 garlic cloves, peeled but left whole
- 8 halves of sun-dried tomatoes in oil, shredded finely
- 2 Tbsp oil from the tomatoes
- Salt and freshly ground black pepper
- 2–3 Tbsp chopped fresh parsley

Preparation time: 10 minutes

Cooking time: 20 minutes
---

❶ Toss the eggplant and onion in the paprika. Heat the oil in a large skillet, add the eggplant and onion and cook for 3 to 4 minutes. Add the garlic and cook for 2 to 3 minutes, then add the tomatoes and their oil.

❷ Continue to stir-fry for 8 to 10 minutes, until the eggplant is tender, and the onion and garlic have caramelized slightly. Season, then add the parsley before serving.

Imam Bayaldi - *the Imam fainted*

Although I have found many differing recipes for this time-honored dish, here's mine! The dish is served cold. The title comes from the legend that the Imam, or holy man, was overcome by the delicious aroma when this was cooked for him!

SERVES 4

- 4 large eggplants
- Salt
- ⅔ cup fruity olive oil
- Juice of 1 lemon
- 1 tsp superfine sugar
- About 2½ cups thick tomato juice
- Chopped fresh parsley, to garnish

STUFFING:

- ½ lb tomatoes, skinned, and chopped
- 1 large onion, finely chopped
- 3 Tbsp chopped fresh parsley
- Salt and freshly ground black pepper
- 1 tsp ground cinnamon

Preparation and salting time:

1½ hours

Cooking time: 1 hour

Chilling time: 2 hours
---

❶ Score the flesh on the eggplants every ½ inch. Pare away alternate strips of skin, to make stripes. Stand the eggplants in a colander, sprinkle with salt and leave for 30 to 60 minutes. Rinse well, then dry.

❷ Combine all the ingredients for the stuffing. Slit the eggplants on one side and pack the stuffing into them, then place in a covered skillet or sauté pan, slit side uppermost.

❸ Pour the oil and lemon juice over the eggplants and sprinkle with the sugar. Add just enough tomato juice to cover them. Cover the pan and simmer slowly for about 1 hour, until the eggplants are soft. Alternatively, bake them for about 1 hour at 325°F.

❹ Season the sauce once the eggplants are cooked, then allow them to cool completely. Chill for about 1 hour, then serve with the tomato sauce spooned over, with a rice salad or lettuce leaves.

vegetable dishes

Imam Bayaldi

Spaghetti with Eggplant and Zucchini

A very simple recipe becomes something special with the addition of pine nuts and eggplant slices.

SERVES 4

- Olive oil, for frying
- ⅓ cup pine nuts
- 1 large eggplant, sliced
- 1 lb spaghetti
- 2 large zucchini, sliced
- 1–2 garlic cloves, crushed
- 2 Tbsp torn basil leaves and chopped fresh parsley, mixed
- Salt and freshly ground black pepper
- Freshly grated Parmesan cheese, to serve

Preparation time: 10 minutes

Cooking time: 20 minutes

---

❶ Bring a large pan of salted water to a boil. Heat a little oil in a large skillet, add the pine nuts and cook until golden. Remove with a slotted spoon and leave on a plate, then add the eggplant with more oil and fry until starting to soften and brown.

❷ Add the pasta to the boiling water, return to a boil and simmer until *al dente* (cooked, that is, until it offers a slight resistance when bitten, but is not soft or overdone).

❸ Add the zucchini and garlic to the skillet and continue frying for 8 to 10 minutes until all the vegetables are soft and golden.

❹ Drain the pasta and add it to the skillet with the herbs. Season to taste. Add the pine nuts and toss well. Serve immediately, with grated Parmesan.

TIP

Fresh pasta cooks in about 2 to 3 minutes, while good-quality dried pasta may take 10 to 12 minutes. You need lots of water and generous amounts of salt. Allow ½ teaspoon of salt to 2 pints of boiling water.

Vegetable Loaf

A really tasty, vegetable loaf. Serve with a tomato or mushroom sauce, or a good spoonful of spicy fruit relish.

- 1 cup brown rice
- 3–4 Tbsp olive oil
- 1 large eggplant, thickly sliced
- 1 large onion
- 2 zucchini
- 2 garlic cloves, crushed
- 2 cups whole wheat bread crumbs
- 1 large egg, beaten
- 1 cup grated Cheddar cheese
- Salt and freshly ground black pepper
- Butter, for greasing
- Relish, to serve

Preparation time: 1 hour

Cooking time: 40 minutes

❶ Cook the rice in a large pan of water until tender. Do not add salt as it will toughen the rice. Drain in a colander.

❷ Preheat the oven to 375°F. Heat 1 to 2 tablespoons of olive oil in a large skillet, add the eggplant slices and fry until just tender. Remove, and allow to cool.

❸ Shred the onion and zucchini. Heat 2 tablespoons of olive oil in a pan, add the vegetables and cook until just tender. Turn into a large bowl and add the rice, garlic, bread crumbs, egg, and cheese. Season to taste and mix thoroughly.

❹ Butter a large loaf pan, about 7 x 3½ x 2½ inches, and line the bottom with baking parchment. Arrange half the eggplant slices in a layer in the bottom of the pan, then top with half the rice mixture. Make a second layer of eggplant in the middle of the loaf and top with the remaining rice, packing it down firmly. Cover with buttered aluminum foil.

❺ Bake the loaf in the preheated oven for 40 minutes. Remove the foil and ease the loaf away from the sides of the tin with a thin-bladed knife. Turn the loaf out onto a warmed serving plate and serve sliced, with relish.

vegetable dishes

103

Eggplant Stuffed with Mushroom and Egg

These stuffed eggplants have a very fresh and delicate flavor. You could serve them with a parsley sauce if you like, although it is a good, low-fat dish on its own.

SERVES 4

- 2 large eggplants
- 2 Tbsp olive oil
- 1 large onion, chopped
- ¼ lb mushrooms, roughly chopped
- 1½ cups well-flavored broth
- 2 Tbsp tomato paste
- 2 hard-cooked eggs, roughly chopped
- 1 Tbsp chopped fresh flat-leaf parsley
- Salt and freshly ground black pepper

Preparation time: 40 minutes

Cooking time: 30 minutes

---

❶ Cut the eggplants in half lengthways, leaving on the stalks to help keep them in shape when they are baking. Carefully scrape out the flesh, leaving a shell about ¼ inch thick. Salt the shells lightly and leave them upside down on paper towels to drain while preparing the filling. Roughly chop the eggplant flesh.

❷ Preheat the oven to 400°F. Heat the oil in a pan. Add the onion and cook until softened but not browned, then add the mushrooms and cook for a further minute. Stir the eggplant flesh into the pan, then add the broth and tomato paste. Bring to a boil, then simmer quite quickly, uncovered, for about 20 minutes.

❸ Rinse the eggplant shells in cold water, then drain well and place in an ovenproof dish. When the eggplant is cooked and the mixture has become a thick sauce, add the chopped eggs and parsley to the sauce, then season to taste.

❹ Divide the filling between the eggplants, then pour a little boiling water into the bottom of the dish. Cover the dish with aluminum foil, then bake for 30 minutes, until the eggplant shells are tender. Serve immediately with freshly cooked green vegetables such as broccoli, zucchini, or peas.

Eggplant and Sweet Potato Curry

This makes a very substantial main course, but it could also be served as a side dish with meat or fish curries.

Serves 4

- 2 tsp cumin seeds
- 1 Tbsp mustard seeds
- 3 Tbsp ghee or sunflower oil
- 2 small sweet potatoes, about 1 lb, peeled and cut into ½-inch chunks
- 1 large onion, finely sliced
- 2 garlic cloves, finely sliced
- 1–2 tsp chili powder
- 1 tsp ground turmeric
- 1 large eggplant, cut the same size as the potato
- 1 Tbsp blue poppy seeds
- 1 cup water or vegetable broth
- 2 tsp salt
- 1 Tbsp torn fresh cilantro leaves

Preparation time: 15 minutes

Cooking time: 45 minutes

❶ Heat a large skillet over a medium heat, then add the cumin and mustard seeds and dry-fry for 30 seconds or so, until aromatic and starting to pop. Transfer to a plate and leave to cool.

❷ Heat the ghee or oil in the pan, add the potatoes and cook for 3 to 4 minutes until starting to soften. Add the onion, garlic, chili powder, and turmeric and cook for 1 to 2 minutes, then add the eggplant with the roasted spices and the poppy seeds. Stir in the water and salt, then cover and simmer very slowly for 30 to 45 minutes, until the vegetables are tender.

❸ Season the curry to taste, then serve sprinkled with the torn cilantro leaves.

Lentil Moussaka

A meatless variation of the classic baked dish. This is rich, filling, and full of fiber, so it must be good for you!

SERVES 4 TO 6

- Olive oil, for frying
- 1 large onion, chopped
- 2 garlic cloves, crushed
- 1 green bell pepper, cored, seeded and chopped
- 2 Tbsp olive oil
- 1 cup red lentils
- About ⅔ cup red wine
- 2 cups canned chopped tomatoes
- Salt and freshly ground black pepper
- 1 Tbsp chopped fresh oregano
- 2 large eggplants, sliced
- 2½ cups milk
- 4 Tbsp butter, plus extra for greasing
- 4 Tbsp all-purpose flour
- 1 cup grated Cheddar cheese

Preparation time: 45 minutes

Cooking time: 30 minutes

❶ Preheat the oven to 425°F. Heat 2 tablespoons of oil in a large pan. Add the onion, garlic, and bell pepper and cook gently until soft. Add the lentils, red wine, and tomatoes. Bring to the boil, then season and add the oregano. Simmer for 20 minutes, or until the lentils are soft. Add a little more wine or stock to the sauce if it seems dry.

❷ Meanwhile, heat 2 to 3 tablespoons of oil in a large skillet. Fry the eggplant slices on both sides until tender, adding more oil if necessary, then drain on paper towels. Add any oil left in the pan to the lentil sauce.

❸ Heat the milk, butter and flour together in a pan, stirring all the time, until boiling and thickened. Continue to cook for 1 minute, to remove the taste of flour from the sauce, then remove the pan from the heat. Add all but 2 tablespoons of the grated cheese. Season to taste.

❹ Layer the lentil sauce and eggplant slices in a buttered, ovenproof dish, finishing with a layer of eggplant. Spoon the cheese sauce over the eggplant, then scatter the remaining cheese over the top. Bake in the preheated oven for 30 minutes, until the moussaka is browned and set. Serve immediately.

vegetable dishes

Nut and Eggplant Sausages

The nuts give a good texture to these sausages. Do cook them slowly, or the nuts will burn and stick.

SERVES 4

- 1 eggplant
- 1½ cups instant potato granules
- 2 cups boiling water
- Salt and freshly ground black pepper
- 6 scallions, very finely chopped
- 2 Tbsp chopped fresh oregano or parsley
- 1 cup mixed chopped nuts
- Flour, if necessary
- 3–4 Tbsp olive oil

Preparation time: 1 hour
Cooking time: 10 minutes
---

❶ Cook the eggplant over a barbecue, under the broiler, or in a hot oven until the skin is wrinkled and blistered, and the flesh is tender, turning from time to time. Cover with a damp cloth, then leave for 10 minutes until cool enough to handle. Peel off the skin.

❷ Mix the potato with the boiling water and add salt and pepper. Purée the eggplant in a food processor, then add it to the potato with the scallions, herbs, and nuts. Shape the mixture into 8 thick sausages.

❸ Heat 2 to 3 tablespoons of olive oil in a large skillet, then fry the sausages gently until lightly browned on all sides. Serve with a blue cheese dressing or fruity relish.

Eggplant and Tomato Gratin

The potatoes in this gratin turn it into a substantial supper dish.

SERVES 4

- Olive oil, for frying
- 2 large eggplants, thickly sliced
- 1 large onion, chopped
- 1 lb potatoes, thickly sliced
- 2 garlic cloves, finely sliced
- Salt and freshly ground black pepper
- 8 ripe tomatoes, sliced
- ⅔ cup well-flavored broth
- 1 cup mixed grated cheeses: Cheddar, blue cheese, mozzarella
- ½ cup fresh bread crumbs

Preparation time: 15 minutes
Cooking time: 40 minutes
---

❶ Heat 2 to 3 tablespoons of the oil in a large pan, add the eggplant slices and fry until lightly browned on both sides. Remove them with a slotted spoon. Add the onion and sliced potatoes to the pan, with a little extra oil if necessary, and cook until starting to soften. Stir in the garlic and season to taste. Return the eggplants to the pan with the sliced tomatoes, add the broth, then cover the pan and cook slowly for 30 minutes, or until all the vegetables are tender. Season.

❷ Turn the vegetables into a buttered, ovenproof gratin dish, with as much of the cooking liquor as you wish. Mix the cheeses with the bread crumbs and scatter over the vegetables. Broil until the cheese has melted and browned. Serve immediately.

Eggplant and Tomato Gratin

Eggplant and Tomato Galette

I like to serve this as a supper dish, but it could easily be stretched to feed more as an appetizer. Although it takes some time to prepare, the work can all be done in advance so that the galette can be baked at the last moment.

SERVES 4

- Butter, for greasing
- 6 large eggs, beaten
- ¼ cup milk
- Salt and freshly ground black pepper
- 1 large eggplant, sliced
- Olive oil, for frying
- 4 tomatoes, sliced
- 1–2 garlic cloves, thinly sliced
- ¼ lb mozzarella, thinly sliced

SAUCE:

- ⅔ cup sour cream
- ⅔ cup thick plain yogurt
- 2 Tbsp chopped chives
- Grated rind and juice of ½ lemon

Preparation time: 45 minutes
Cooking time: 25 minutes
---

❶ Preheat the oven to 400°F, and butter a round gratin dish, the same diameter as your omelet pan. Beat the eggs with the milk and a little seasoning, then use to make 3 fairly thick omelets. Stack the finished omelets on paper towels until required. (I finish the top of each omelet under a hot broiler, to save turning them over in the pan.)

❷ Heat 2 to 3 tablespoons of olive oil in a skillet. Add the eggplant and cook until just tender and lightly browned, adding more oil as necessary. Place one omelet in the bottom of the buttered dish, then arrange half the eggplant slices in a layer on top. Season lightly, then cover with half the sliced tomatoes and garlic. Season again and top with a third of the mozzarella. Repeat the layers, finishing with an omelet topped with mozzarella.

❸ Bake in the preheated oven for 20 to 25 minutes, until the galette is piping hot and the mozzarella has melted and is lightly browned.

❹ Mix all the ingredients for the sauce together while the galette is baking. Serve the galette cut into quarters, with the sauce spooned over and around it.

Eggplant and Wild Rice Bake

I love casseroles of wild rice, so for this recipe I decided to make a thick casserole which would give a fragrant, moist filling between layers of eggplant.

SERVES 4

- About 6 Tbsp olive oil
- 1 large onion, finely chopped
- 1–2 garlic cloves, crushed
- 1 large carrot, finely chopped
- 1 green bell pepper, cored, seeded and chopped
- 1 cup wild rice
- 2 cups chopped tomatoes
- 1 cup well-flavored broth
- 2 large eggplants, thickly sliced
- 1 Tbsp chopped fresh oregano
- Salt and freshly ground black pepper
- ¼ lb soft goat cheese, crumbled (optional)

Preparation time: 1 hour

Cooking time: 20 minutes

❶ Heat 2 tablespoons of oil in a pan. Add the onion and garlic and cook until softened but not browned, then add the carrot and cook for a further 2 minutes or so. Stir in the pepper and rice, then add the chopped tomatoes and stock. Bring to a boil, then cover the pan and simmer for 50 to 60 minutes, or until the rice is tender.

❷ Meanwhile, heat 3 to 4 tablespoons of olive oil in a griddle pan or skillet. Add the eggplant slices and cook lightly on both sides. Add

more oil as necessary, but try not to use too much as this is otherwise a fairly low-fat recipe. Preheat the oven to 375°F.

❸ Layer half the eggplant slices in the bottom of an ovenproof dish. Add the chopped oregano to the rice, then season to taste. Pour the rice over the eggplant, then top with the remaining slices. Season lightly and crumble the goat cheese over the top, if using. Bake in the preheated oven for 20 minutes. Serve with a green salad.

TIP

Wild rice, harvested only in America, and in fact a type of grass seed, has a nutty flavor. It gives a luxurious touch to create a special meal.

vegetable dishes

111

Tortillas Stuffed with Eggplant and Chile

Flour tortillas are easy to use and can turn almost any combination of ingredients into a quick Tex Mex meal. You could used chopped scallions or avocado as additional salad garnishes. Leave the chile unseeded if you like your tortillas hot.

SERVES 4

- 1 large eggplant, cut into ½-inch chunks
- 1 onion, finely chopped
- 1 tsp chili powder
- ⅓ cup groundnut oil
- 1 green chile, seeded and chopped
- 1 garlic clove, finely chopped
- ½ cup pecan nuts, roughly chopped
- 8 flour tortillas, warmed in a microwave or in the oven

TO SERVE:

- Grated Cheddar cheese
- Shredded lettuce
- Chopped tomatoes
- Sour cream

Preparation time: 10 minutes

Cooking time: 15 minutes

---

❶ Toss the eggplant and onion in the chili powder. Heat the oil in a large skillet, add the eggplant and onion, and fry gently until lightly browned on all sides, about 5 minutes. Add the chile, garlic, and pecans and continue cooking for a further 5 minutes, or until all the vegetables are tender.

❷ Meanwhile, heat the flour tortillas, either in the oven or in a microwave according to the instructions on the packet.

❸ To serve, place some of the eggplant mixture in the center of each tortilla, then top with a little cheese, lettuce, sour cream, and tomatoes. Fold the bottom of the tortilla upwards, then roll the sides over to enclose the filling.

vegetable dishes

Chickpea and Eggplant Stew

A rich vegetable stew with a sesame-flavored sauce and a crisp salsa garnish.
I suggest serving this with garlic bread and a green leaf salad.

SERVES 4

- 1 cup chickpeas, soaked overnight
- ¼ cup olive oil
- 1 large onion, finely sliced
- 2 eggplants, sliced
- Grated rind and juice of 1 lemon
- 1–2 garlic cloves, finely sliced
- 1 cup dry white wine
- 2 cups broth
- Salt and freshly ground black pepper
- 2 bay leaves
- 4 Tbsp chopped fresh mixed herbs, such as flat-leaf parsley, marjoram, oregano, tarragon etc.
- 4 Tbsp tahini paste

SALSA:

- 1 orange
- 2 tomatoes, chopped
- ½ cucumber, chopped
- 1 red onion, finely chopped
- 1 Tbsp chopped fresh parsley

Preparation time: 20 minutes
plus overnight soaking
Cooking time: 1½ hours

---

❶ Drain the chickpeas and rinse them thoroughly. Place in a large pan with enough water to cover and bring to a boil. Boil rapidly for 10 minutes, then reduce the heat and leave to simmer slowly.

❷ Meanwhile, heat the oil in a pan. Add the onion and eggplant and cook until softened and just starting to brown; do not add any extra oil as this dish will be quite rich. Drain the chickpeas and add to the pan with the grated lemon rind, garlic, wine, and broth. Stir well, add the seasonings, then bring to a boil. Cover and simmer slowly for 1 hour, or until the chickpeas are tender.

❸ While the chickpeas are cooking, prepare the salsa. Pare the rind from the orange and place it in a bowl. Peel the fruit, then chop the flesh into small dice. Add all the remaining salsa ingredients. Season to taste, then allow to stand.

❹ Stir the tahini into the chickpea mixture, then season well. Serve in deep plates, with a good spoonful of salsa on each helping.

vegetable dishes

114

Eggplant and Fennel Relish

Sweet Eggplant and Mango Chutney

Eggplants Preserved with Mint

Eggplant Salsa with Tomatoes

Eggplant and Mint Relish

Eggplant-stuffed Parathas

Indian-Style Eggplant Relish

Mustard Seed and Eggplant Salsa

Warm Eggplant and Zucchini Salsa

Eggplant and Walnut Bread

Eggplant and Nutmeg Ice Cream

Eggplant and Fennel Relish

I have added some fresh fennel to the eggplant in this Arabic-style relish, which provides a little contrast in texture. Fennel and eggplant have very complementary flavors. This is a relish which looks well in a preserving jar.

MAKES ABOUT 4½ LB

- 2¼ lb small young eggplants, halved and cut into 2-inch chunks
- Salt
- 2 Tbsp coriander seeds
- 2 Tbsp fennel seeds
- About 1½ cups fruity olive oil
- 1 fennel bulb, finely sliced
- Fine sea salt
- 2 Tbsp black peppercorns
- ½ cup red wine vinegar

Preparation time: 1 hour for salting
Cooking time: 15 minutes

❶ Layer the eggplants in a colander with salt and leave for at least 1 hour. Rinse thoroughly under cold running water, then pat dry on paper towels.

❷ Heat a large skillet over a moderate heat, then add the coriander and fennel seeds and dry-fry them for about 30 seconds, until fragrant and starting to brown. Transfer to a plate and leave to cool.

❸ Heat ½ cup of olive oil in the skillet, then add the eggplant and fennel and cook for about 5 minutes, until the eggplant is lightly browned. Remove with a slotted spoon and allow to drain on paper towels.

❹ Pack the eggplant and fennel into warmed preserving jars, seasoning the layers lightly with salt and packing the vegetables pieces down firmly with the back of a spoon. Scatter each layer with the toasted seeds mixed with peppercorns.

❺ Mix any oil remaining in the skillet with the vinegar and sufficient olive oil to cover the vegetables: the mixture should be about one part vinegar to two parts oil. Seal the jars, then leave in a cool, dark place for about a week before serving. Eat within 4 to 6 weeks. Always store in the refrigerator.

Sweet Eggplant and Mango Chutney

This is a sweet but hot chutney, ideal for serving with curries, or with bread and cheese at a picnic lunch.

- 4 small green mangoes, ripe but firm, peeled and cut into chunks
- 2 eggplants, cut into 1-inch chunks
- 2–3 garlic cloves, crushed
- 2 hot red chiles, finely chopped
- ¾ cup finely chopped fresh ginger
- 1 Tbsp chili powder
- 1 Tbsp coarse sea salt
- 2½ cups malt vinegar
- 5½ cups light brown sugar

Preparation time: 10 minutes
plus 1 hour for salting
Cooking time: 1 hour

❶ Layer the mangoes and eggplants in a colander, salting them lightly. Leave for 1 hour, then rinse well in cold water and drain.

❷ Place the mangoes and eggplants in a large pan with all the remaining ingredients. Bring slowly to a boil, then cook gently for 45 to 60 minutes, until the chutney is well reduced but still juicily moist.

❸ Pour into warmed jars, packing the mixture well down, then seal and label. Leave for 3 to 4 weeks to mature before eating.

relishes and accompaniments

117

Eggplants Preserved with Mint

Try to use preserving jars for this recipe, as they make excellent presents. The eggplants must remain completely covered by the oil to be properly preserved.

MAKES ABOUT 4¼ LB

- 2¼ lb small eggplants
- Salt
- 2½ cups white wine vinegar
- 6–8 garlic cloves, according to size, finely sliced
- ¾ cup fresh mint leaves, left whole
- 1 Tbsp mixed peppercorns
- 2 large green chiles, seeded and finely shredded
- 2 cups fruity olive oil

Preparation time: 2–3 hours
or overnight for salting
Cooking time: 15 minutes

---

❶ Cut the eggplants into quarters lengthwise, then into 2-inch chunks. Layer them in a colander with plenty of salt. Leave to stand for 2 to 3 hours, or overnight. Rinse thoroughly, then drain and shake dry.

❷ Bring the vinegar to a boil in a deep pan, then add the eggplants and garlic and boil for 5 minutes. Stir once or twice, to keep the eggplants covered with the vinegar. Drain and allow to cool completely.

❸ Layer the eggplants and garlic alternately with the mint in warm, clean preserving jars. Season each layer with a mixture of the

peppercorns and sliced chiles, and pack the layers tightly by pressing down firmly with a wooden spoon.

❹ Pour half the oil into the jars, to just cover the eggplants, then cover and leave overnight. By the next day, the eggplants will have absorbed much of the oil. Add sufficient extra oil to cover the eggplants completely, then seal the jar and leave for at least a week before serving.

Eggplant Salsa with Tomatoes

Most salsas are made with raw vegetables and fruits, so this is an unusual combination of half cooked and half raw vegetables. Use a yellow bell pepper for color if yellow tomatoes are not available.

SERVES 4

- 4 Tbsp fruity olive oil
- 1 large eggplant, cut into ¼-inch dice
- 1 red onion, finely chopped
- 4 red tomatoes, seeded and chopped
- 2 yellow tomatoes, seeded and chopped
- 1 green chile, seeded and finely chopped
- 1 avocado, peeled and cut into ½-inch chunks
- Grated rind and juice of 1 lime
- Salt and freshly ground black pepper
- 3 Tbsp freshly chopped cilantro

Preparation time: 10 minutes

Cooking time: 10 minutes

---

❶ Heat the oil in a pan. Add the eggplant and cook until browned and tender, then remove with a slotted spoon and place in a salad bowl. Allow the eggplant to cool. Reserve any oil left in the pan.

❷ Add all the remaining ingredients to the bowl, tossing the avocado in the lime juice. Season well, then finally stir in any remaining oil and the cilantro leaves. Allow to stand before serving, to allow the flavors to blend.

Eggplant and Mint Relish

This is almost a vegetable sauce, but the ingredients are chunky. It is excellent with kabobs or lentil patties. Remove the chile seeds for a cooler relish.

SERVES 4 TO 6

- 4 Tbsp fruity olive oil
- 1 large onion, finely chopped
- 1 eggplant, cut into ½-inch dice
- 2 garlic cloves, finely chopped
- 2 large green bell peppers, cored, seeded and cut into ¼-inch dice
- 1 red chile, finely sliced
- 1 Tbsp white wine vinegar
- Salt and freshly ground black pepper
- Sugar, to taste

Preparation time: 10 minutes

Cooking time: 10 minutes

---

❶ Heat the oil in a pan, add the onion and eggplant and cook until tender and lightly browned. Add the garlic and bell peppers, and continue cooking for a further 2 minutes, until the peppers are slightly softened.

❷ Remove the pan from the heat and stir in the chile – it has more impact if added raw. Turn the relish into a serving dish, then add the vinegar and season to taste, adding a little sugar if necessary. Serve the relish warm or cold.

relishes and accompaniments

Eggplant-stuffed Parathas

These flatbreads are almost a meal in themselves. Serve with any spiced dish, or as a tasty snack in their own right.

MAKES 6

- 3 cups fine whole wheat flour, plus extra for dusting
- ½ tsp salt
- About 1¼ cups water
- Vegetable oil or melted ghee, for frying
- 1–2 Tbsp butter
- Yogurt or relish, to serve

FILLING:

- 3 Tbsp vegetable or peanut oil
- 1 eggplant, cut into ¼-inch dice
- ½ tsp chili powder
- ½ tsp ground turmeric
- 1 Tbsp finely chopped fresh ginger
- 2 green chiles, seeded and finely chopped
- 2 Tbsp chopped fresh cilantro
- 1 tsp salt

Preparation time: 30 minutes

Cooking time: 15 minutes

---

❶ First make the filling. Heat the oil in a pan. Add the eggplant with the chili powder and turmeric and cook until soft, then add the remaining ingredients for the filling and mix well. Remove from the heat and leave to cool.

❷ Mix the flour and salt to a firm, manageable dough with cold water, then knead until pliable. Cover with a bowl and leave for 10 minutes.

❸ Divide the dough into 6 pieces. Work with one piece of dough at a time, leaving the others covered until required. Roll out to a circle about 4 inches in diameter, then place some filling on the dough. Fold the edges over to enclose the filling, then dip the dough in a little extra flour and roll it out into a circle about 7 inches in diameter. The eggplant may break through the dough; try not to press too hard on the edges of the dough when rolling. If necessary, sprinkle a little extra flour over the dough to hold the filling.

❹ Heat a griddle or large skillet over a moderate heat, then cook the parathas briefly for about 1 minute on each side. Brush each side with melted ghee or oil and cook gently until lightly browned and crisp. Keep the parathas warm wrapped in a clean cloth in a very low oven until they are all cooked. Serve hot, dotted with butter and with a spoonful of yogurt or relish.

Indian-style Eggplant Relish

Most Indian relishes contain a large quantity of oil and are very hot, and this is no exception. It is an excellent relish to add in small quantities to shrimp curries.

MAKES ABOUT 2¼ LB

- 1 lb firm young eggplants, cut into 1-inch chunks
- Salt
- 1 Tbsp cumin seeds
- 1¼ cups groundnut oil
- 2 large onions, chopped
- 4 garlic cloves, finely chopped
- 2-inch piece fresh ginger, peeled and finely chopped
- 1 tsp ground turmeric
- 2 Tbsp light brown sugar
- 4 hot red chiles, finely sliced
- 2 green chiles, finely sliced

Preparation time: 10 minutes

plus 1 hour for salting

Cooking time: 10 minutes

---

❶ Layer the eggplants in a colander with salt and leave for at least 1 hour. Rinse thoroughly under cold running water, then pat dry on paper towels.

❷ Heat a large skillet over moderate heat, then add the cumin seeds and dry fry them for 30 seconds, until fragrant and just starting to color. Tip onto a plate and leave to cool.

❸ Heat the oil in the skillet. Add the eggplants and onion and cook for 3 to 4 minutes, then add the garlic, ginger, and turmeric and continue cooking for a further 2 minutes. Allow to cool slightly, then mix the sugar into the oil with 1 teaspoon of salt.

❹ Pack the eggplants and onions into warmed jars, layering them with the sliced chiles. Press down firmly on each layer with the back of a spoon to exclude all air from the jars. Pour as much of the oil into the jars as possible, then seal.

❺ Keep the pickles for at least 2 to 3 weeks before using; a month or so is better still. Store in the refrigerator to keep them cold, and use quickly once opened.

Mustard Seed and Eggplant Salsa

Roasting some spices to add to a salsa not only gives extra flavor, but texture too. The combination of eggplant, mustard seeds and orange here is especially good.

SERVES 4

- 1 Tbsp white mustard seeds
- 4 Tbsp olive oil
- 1 eggplant, cut into ¼-inch dice
- 1 large orange
- 2 tomatoes, seeded and chopped
- 4 scallions, finely chopped
- ½ cucumber, cut into ¼-inch dice
- 2 rings of pineapple, cut into chunks
- Salt and freshly ground black pepper
- 2 Tbsp chopped fresh parsley

Preparation time: 10 minutes

Cooking time: 15 minutes

❶ Heat a large skillet over a medium heat, then add the mustard seeds and dry fry for about 30 seconds, until they are just fragrant. Turn into a salad bowl.

❷ Heat the oil in the skillet, add the eggplant and cook until lightly browned and tender. Transfer the eggplant to the salad bowl with a slotted spoon and leave until cold.

❸ Pare the rind from the orange and add it to the bowl, then peel and chop the fruit. Add the orange to the eggplant with the remaining ingredients and season. Add the parsley to the bowl, then allow to stand for 30 minutes before serving.

Warm Eggplant and Zucchini Salsa

This is really a warm salad, so serve immediately. If kept warm, the vegetables will stew and the texture will be ruined.

SERVES 4

- 3 Tbsp pine nuts
- About 4 Tbsp olive oil
- 1 large eggplant, cut into ¼-inch dice
- 2 zucchini, cut into ¼-inch dice
- 4 tomatoes, seeded and diced
- 1 large yellow bell pepper, cored, seeded, and cut into ¼-inch dice
- 2 garlic cloves, finely shredded
- 12 basil leaves, finely shredded
- A few drops of balsamic vinegar
- Salt and freshly ground black pepper

Preparation time: 10 minutes

Cooking time: 10 minutes

❶ Heat a large skillet over a medium heat. Add the pine nuts and dry-fry for about 1 minute, tossing until they are golden brown. Remove from the skillet and keep to one side on a plate.

❷ Heat 4 tablespoons of oil in the skillet. Add the eggplant and cook for 2 minutes, then add the zucchini and continue cooking until the vegetables are tender, adding more oil if necessary.

❸ Stir the remaining ingredients into the skillet and add the pine nuts. Season to taste and serve immediately.

Eggplant and Walnut Bread

The perfect picnic loaf to serve with a tomato and feta cheese salad. The loaf is much better made with fresh yeast if at all possible.

MAKES 1 LARGE LOAF

- ½ oz fresh yeast or 1 Tbsp dried fast-acting yeast
- 1½ cups tepid water
- 4 cups strong white bread flour
- 1 cup whole wheat flour
- 1 Tbsp salt
- 2 Tbsp walnut oil
- ½ cup roughly chopped walnuts

FILLING:

- 1 large eggplant, finely sliced
- 1 onion, finely sliced
- 3–4 Tbsp walnut oil
- 1 tsp ground cinnamon
- 3 Tbsp seedless raisins
- Salt and freshly ground black pepper

Preparation time: 3 hours
Cooking time: 35 minutes

---

❶ Crumble the fresh yeast into the warm water and leave for 3 to 4 minutes, then stir until dissolved. If using dried yeast, mix with the flour. Mix the flours and salt together in a large bowl, then add the yeast liquid, or water if using dried yeast, and mix to a dough. Turn out onto a floured surface and punch down for 10 minutes, until the dough is elastic in texture. Return the dough to the bowl, cover and leave in a warm place for about 1 hour, or until doubled in size.

❷ Meanwhile, prepare the filling. Heat the walnut oil in a pan, add the eggplant and onion and cook with the cinnamon until browned on all sides. Stir in the raisins, then season with salt and pepper and allow to cool completely.

❸ Knock back the dough and reshape it, then return it to the bowl and leave covered for a further 30 minutes in a warm place.

❹ Lightly flour a cookie sheet. Knock the dough back again, then knead in the chopped walnuts and divide the dough into 3 pieces. Roll the dough into 3 circles about 8 inches in diameter. Place one circle on the floured cookie sheet, top with half the filling then repeat the layers again, finishing with the last piece of dough. Seal the edges of the dough together with a little water, then cover with a damp cloth and leave in a warm place for 45 minutes to rise again. Preheat the oven to 475°F.

❺ Bake the bread on the cookie sheet in the preheated oven for 30 to 35 minutes, until browned and well risen. Remove from the oven and leave to cool on a wire rack. Serve with a tomato and feta cheese salad.

Eggplant and Nutmeg Ice Cream

Probably my most unusual ice-cream to date! Try it—it really is delicious.

SERVES 4 TO 6

- 1 small eggplant, sliced
- Superfine or granulated sugar, for sprinkling

Vanilla syrup:

- 1¼ cups granulated sugar
- 1 vanilla bean
- 1 cup water
- 4 green cardamoms, lightly crushed

Ice Cream:

- 1¼ cups milk
- 1 vanilla bean
- 4 large egg yolks
- ⅓ cup superfine sugar
- Freshly grated nutmeg, to taste— I use about half a nutmeg
- 1¼ cups heavy cream

Preparation time: 10–12 hours for the eggplant plus 2–3 hours for ice cream

Freezing time: 25 minutes in an ice-cream machine or 4–5 hours in a freezer

---

❶ Arrange the eggplant slices in a single layer on a cookie sheet and sprinkle generously with sugar. Leave for 1 hour, so that any bitter juices are extracted.

❷ Prepare the vanilla syrup. Place the ingredients in a small pan and bring gently to a boil, stirring all the time until the sugar is dissolved. Boil for 10 to 15 minutes, until the syrup is well reduced. Meanwhile, rinse the eggplant slices thoroughly, then drain and dry on paper towels. Place the slices in the hot syrup. Remove the pan from the heat, cover and leave for 1 to 2 hours.

❸ Bring the eggplant slices to a boil in the syrup and simmer for 5 minutes. Leave to cool in the covered pan, then allow to stand for at least 8 hours, or overnight.

❹ Heat the milk with the second vanilla bean until almost at a boil, then cover and leave to stand, off the heat, for at least 20 minutes. Remove the vanilla bean and rinse well—it can be used again to flavor sugar. Beat the egg yolks with the sugar in a bowl until thick and pale. Reheat the milk until almost boiling, then pour it onto the eggs, whisking all the time, then add the nutmeg to taste. Rinse the milk pan in cold water, then return the custard to it and heat gently, until the mixture is just thick enough to coat the back of a wooden spoon. Turn the custard into a clean bowl and leave to cool

completely. Chill for at least an hour before completing the ice cream.

❺ Fold the cream into the custard, then turn into an ice cream maker and freeze-churn until thick. Alternatively, freeze in a suitable plastic container for 4 to 5 hours, stirring the ice cream once or twice. Whip the cream before adding it to the custard if you do not use an ice-cream machine.

❻ Drain the eggplant slices to remove as much syrup as possible, then chop them very finely. Stir the eggplant into the ice cream just before it is ready.

❼ Freshly churned ice cream will need to harden in the freezer for 20 minutes before serving. Frozen ice cream must be tempered before it is suitable for serving. Allow about 20 minutes at normal room temperature.

Index

ACKNOWLEDGEMENTS

The publishers would like to thank West Dean Gardens of Chichester, Sussex, for opening their greenhouses for the photography featured on pages 6 through 14.